THE RETURN OF NATURE

STUDIES IN CONTINENTAL THOUGHT
John Sallis, editor

CONSULTING EDITORS

Robert Bernasconi James Risser
John D. Caputo Dennis J. Schmidt
David Carr Calvin O. Schrag
Edward S. Casey Charles E. Scott
David Farrell Krell Daniela Vallega-Neu
Lenore Langsdorf David Wood

INDIANA UNIVERSITY PRESS
Bloomington & Indianapolis

The Return *of* Nature

ON THE BEYOND OF SENSE

JOHN SALLIS

This book is a publication of

Indiana University Press
Office of Scholarly Publishing
Herman B Wells Library 350
1320 East 10th Street
Bloomington, Indiana 47405 USA

iupress.indiana.edu

© 2016 by John Sallis
All rights reserved

No part of this book may be reproduced or utilized in any form or by any means, electronic or mechanical, including photocopying and recording, or by any information storage and retrieval system, without permission in writing from the publisher. The Association of American University Presses' Resolution on Permissions constitutes the only exception to this prohibition.

The paper used in this publication meets the minimum requirements of the American National Standard for Information Sciences—Permanence of Paper for Printed Library Materials, ANSI Z39.48-1992.

Manufactured in the United States of America

Library of Congress Cataloging-in-Publication Data

Names: Sallis, John, 1938- author.
Title: The return of nature : coming as if from nowhere / John Sallis.
Description: Bloomington : Indiana University Press, 2016. | Series: Studies in Continental thought | Includes bibliographical references and index.
Identifiers: LCCN 2016010956 (print) | LCCN 2016030782 (ebook) | ISBN 9780253022899 (cloth : alk. paper) | ISBN 9780253023131 (pbk. : alk. paper) | ISBN 9780253023377 (ebook)
Subjects: LCSH: Philosophy of nature.
Classification: LCC BD581 .S243 2016 (print) | LCC BD581 (ebook) | DDC 113—dc23
LC record available at https://lccn.loc.gov/2016010956

1 2 3 4 5   21 20 19 18 17 16

There are moments in our lives when we extend a kind of love and tender respect to nature in plants, minerals, animals, and landscapes, as well as to human nature in children, in the customs of country folk and the primitive world, not because it pleases our senses, not even because it satisfies our understanding or taste . . . , but merely *because it is nature.*

    Friedrich Schiller, *Über naïve und sentimentalische Dichtung*

CONTENTS

Acknowledgments   *ix*

PROLOGUE   1

1 THE RETURN OF NATURE   5

2 THE BIRTH OF NATURE   28

3 RETURN TO NATURE   44

4 RETURN FROM THE NATURE BEYOND NATURE   60

5 THE ELEMENTAL TURN   73

6 THE COSMOLOGICAL TURN   81

7 COMING AS IF FROM NOWHERE   92

8 THE PLURALITY OF NATURE AND THE
   DISINTEGRATION OF DIFFERENCE   104

English Index   *121*
Greek Index   *123*

ACKNOWLEDGMENTS

For permission to draw on previously published material, I am grateful to the editors/publishers of the following journals: *Internationales Jahrbuch für Hermeneutik*, *Southern Journal of Philosophy*, and *Journal of Speculative Philosophy*. Thanks also to the editor and publisher of *Phenomenological Perspectives on Plurality*.

All translations are my own.

I am grateful to Nancy Fedrow, Ryan Brown, and Stephen Mendelsohn for their fine assistance during production of this book. The support that my editor and friend Dee Mortensen has provided for the present project has been indispensable, and I am especially grateful to her.

Boston
May 2016

THE RETURN OF NATURE

PROLOGUE

The way along which nature returns from its destitution may lead it to itself, to nature itself, to nature as it itself is, perhaps even as it is in its fullness, as when from the dead of winter nature is reborn in the abundance of its growth. Or it may return in a guise other than that proper to it; it may return in such disguise that it itself, it as it is in itself, is barely to be recognized, as when it is disfigured by forces alien to it, forces that, even if they seem to stem from nature, are contrary to those that belong to it by nature. The way on which nature returns, the cycle of the seasons, for instance, is finely articulated: it is not just a course on which nature circles endlessly but also one that is measured and marked by the phases of nature's withdrawal and return. Nature returns also along a course that is entwined with that of the seasons, the course marked by the nocturnal withdrawal of light and its return with the coming of day by which visibility is restored to all things. On this course each segment has its distinctive character: the colors of dawn, the burst of light at sunrise, the freshness of the morning, the intensity of high noon, the fading light and long shadows of late afternoon—and on toward dusk, the coolness and dampness of night, and on clear nights the appearance of stars, and always the withdrawal of terrestrial things into nocturnal obscurity. On other occasions, for instance, when the weather is unsettled, when thick clouds block the direct sunlight and a cold wind sweeps across the landscape, the course of day and night is articulated in quite a different manner; but regardless of the conditions, this course is measured and marked by the phases in which nature withdraws and returns.

There are occasions, even entire eras, when human intervention drives nature itself to recede behind the fabrications constructed from it. Eventual dereliction may open the space for nature itself to return. Or persistent exploitation may block its return as itself, may allow it to return only as a ghost of what it otherwise would be. Or a theoretical stance oriented to all that would be entirely and invariably itself may posit nature itself beyond nature as it is displayed before our senses; as such, this nature beyond nature will be set beyond all possibility of return and will be regarded as merely imaged by the nature that lies before us, which is thus reduced to a mere remote semblance of nature as it itself, in its utter selfsameness, is.

The return *of* nature may evoke a return *to* nature. With the coming of spring, as we catch sight of the first buds, the tiny leaves, and the other traces of all that will soon arrive, we are enticed by the visible promise of abundance and perhaps even impelled to venture into the surrounding nature. Likewise, it is with the return of light in the morning that we are prompted to set out as the day requires, leaving the shelter that secured us in the night, advancing into the midst of the elements that both embrace us and threaten us. We are perhaps most compellingly drawn to nature when the shining of the things of nature exceeds both our grasp and our words. The beauty of nature may, then, prove to outstrip even that of which art is capable. Indeed, one might imagine a paradigmatic scene in which a person with a genuine sense of beauty would take leave of the museum in order to venture into the open expanse where he might linger before the beauty of nature.

Yet, in order for the splendor of beautiful nature to exercise its attraction, it must become manifest. Indeed, the attraction and the retraction of nature can be displayed before us only if the things of nature become manifest as they are gathered into nature's return and withdrawal. They must show themselves in such a manner that they can be apprehended by sense along with whatever comes to the aid of sense, whatever comes to complete what sense alone can never quite achieve. One of the names that have been given to that which comes to supplement sense is *imagination*. Only through the coming of imagination is it possible to apprehend natural things (animals, flowers, grasses, stones) as well as things fabricated from nature (architectural edifices, utensils of all sorts, instruments for various purposes). Only through the coming of imagination can such things be displayed before us, either as they cohere within the return and withdrawal of nature or as (in the case of fabricated things) they are set at the limit of nature.

Yet, within nature there is gathered not only the configuration of things but also the elements that encompass them: rain and snow, mountains and valleys, wind and sunlight, and, most comprehensively, earth and sky, which delimit the enchorial space in which everything of nature comes to pass. Since the things of nature are encompassed by various elements—and always by earth and sky—they can be apprehended in the fullness of their appearance only if they show themselves within their elemental setting, only if an openness to the elements belongs intrinsically to their apprehension. For an analysis of manifestation as such, it is imperative to carry out a turn to the elements; that is, such an analysis must turn to the elements in order to demonstrate the ways in which the things of nature are encompassed by the elements. If, beyond this elemental turn, the analysis is to be extended to the still broader expanse of the cosmos, then a corresponding cosmological turn is also imperative. Such an extension may be regarded as an enlargement of the sense of nature. Or it may be understood as passage across the limit that separates—yet also conjoins—nature and the cosmos; this limit is determined as the boundary where the encompassing sky is transformed into the enormously expansive cosmos.

Just as the coming of imagination is necessary for the full apprehension of natural things as they appear before sense, so its coming is required also for the openness to the elements that belongs to full apprehension. For even if one occupies a fabricated or even natural enclosure—an edifice or a cave—earth, sky, and the space they delimit will continue to be implicated in one's apprehension of things, and indeed in virtually all the modes of comportment that can be assumed. In every case, openness to the elemental, even if covert, belongs to the apprehension of the things of nature and even of the things fabricated from nature. As imagination comes to let things appear in their elemental setting, it also traces out the spacings of the elementals, which constitute the mobile structure of nature at large.

Nature is also the scene of life. It is nature that sustains and shelters living things, no matter how mediated these means may, as with humans, become. Even when the natural abodes that shelter animals come to be replaced by fabricated enclosures, nature supplies the material of the latter, and the earth provides the support that lets a humanly constructed edifice stand firm. Nature is the scene of growth, the place where living creatures prosper and also suffer decline and death. The Greek designation for what we call nature, φύσις, is linked to the verb φύω, which, among its several senses, means *to grow*. Another of its senses (in the passive-middle form) is *to be born*, and φύσις, as one of its several meanings, means *birth*. Nature is the place of birth, the place where a new life can come to be, a life that never before was, a life that—at least in the case of humans—is from the moment of birth a self to come. Whatever is born—above all, in the case of humans—is singular.

To be attentive to nature and to free it from all that, from beyond nature, would impose on it an alien order is also to protect the singularity that abounds in nature.

The elemental, which gives nature its shape, is also the site of the mythical. Beyond their surface the elements unfold a depth from which the mythical figures can—and to the Greeks did—appear. In the discourse that follows, mythical figures are sometimes woven into the fabric, especially when it touches on the elemental, on imagination, and indeed on the very weaving—and unweaving—of a text. Some of these figures are called by name, most notably Apollo and Penelope. Others, such as Artemis and Aphrodite, remain unnamed. With these various figures, with their veiled passage through the text, what, above all, is in play is the coming of imagination.

1 THE RETURN OF NATURE

Nature returns in many ways. Some ways are open for all to see; they mark returns belonging to nature itself, returns of nature to itself. Other ways are more hidden; because we humans are entwined in the provocation of these returns, because, accordingly, we lack the detachment that clear sight requires, these ways are elusive. Exceptional circumspection is needed in order to discern and retrace them.

There are no ways of return to which human senses and sensibilities are more attuned than those marked by the seasons. Unquestionably preeminent among these is nature's return to itself in spring. With the coming of spring, it is as though, having endured the dead of winter, nature were now reborn. The snow, if it still remains, begins to recede, and patches of ground appear covered with brown vegetation and soaked from the melt. The days lengthen. The chill of the winter wind is gone. One feels the warmth of the sun as its itinerary across the sky moves ever higher from the horizon. Birds return and charm us with their repertoire of songs. The advent of spring restores nature's vitality and ushers in new growth. On bare branches buds, blossoms, and tiny leaves appear, and the haze of fine, lacy green that gradually begins to form already holds out the promise of the fullness that in summer will finally return. In this sense, then, summer too marks a return of nature. It brings the full heat of the sun and the longest days of the year, the lush and varied vegetation, the profusion of flowers, the abundance of wild creatures—rabbits, squirrels, woodchucks—to be seen in the countryside, and, toward the end of the season, the nocturnal symphonies of crickets and locusts. If indeed fall and winter mark the retreat from which nature will again return, even they also signal particular kinds of return, fall the return of nature's most brilliant colors, winter the return of the stillness of snow.

Equally evocative is the return of the day, of dawn and the first rays of sunlight, which promise a new day and the possibilities it opens up. Since the lengths of day and night vary inversely in the course of the year, the cycle of day and night is entwined with that of the seasons. Both serve to measure out time, to mark its elemental advance.

The cycle of the seasons and the returns of nature bound up with it vary, of course, from one region of the earth to another. The description here is geared to temperate regions such as the United States and western and central Europe. As one approaches the equator, the differences diminish yet do not disappear entirely. As one travels to the north, the differences become greater, especially in extent as winter extends over a much larger portion of the year. The difference between the lengths of day and night reaches its extreme—in northern Canada and northern Scandinavia—with the midnight sun of midsummer and the almost total darkness of midwinter.

Nature returns also when a site once cleared by humans is abandoned. Around the ruins of an ancient castle, which, set on the mountainside, once offered the sovereign a view over the entire valley, nature has now encroached. Vines have crept over the stones that remain, and in what was once its courtyard grasses and scrub now grow freely. Around its entire perimeter the forest has advanced, returning to the site from which it was once cleared away. The view of the valley below, once enjoyed by the sovereign, is now almost completely blocked by saplings that have taken root in front of the ruins. Even from the one high wall that remains, a number of stones have fallen out and now lie on the ground, many covered with moss, all in the process of returning to nature, all caught up in the return of nature.

Nature returns also within the expanse of history. When art and thought wander too far from nature, when they come to rely too exclusively on human artifice, the call will inevitably be sounded for a return of nature and a return to nature. The nobility of a humanity unsullied by the repressive and artificial conventions of civilization will be sought. The appearance of beauty will be apprehended, not in the creations fashioned by humans, but in the exuberance of nature. The affirmation of nature will be enacted by recourse to an abode set within the things of nature. Not only the philosopher but also the artist, the poet, and the naturalist will have recourse to nature in such a way as to broach a return of nature and an affirmation of the belonging of the human to nature. In their texts and their works, each will strive to present both the beauty and the force of nature.

In certain of the ways in which nature returns, we humans cannot escape being engaged. There are occasions when nature lets its beauty appear, when it shines forth in a scene so wondrous that it draws us into a contemplative repose in which we linger before the scene, rapt in our attunement to it while borne on by the play of imagination. When it turns this aspect to us, it returns to our vision in a different guise and thus to a vision that surpasses the everyday perception that preceded it, to a vision that is evoked precisely and only by the beautiful scene. And yet, there are also occasions when the very nature in which we normally live with some contentment turns another side to us and returns in a more sinister guise so as to threaten or even assault us, replacing beauty not just with ugliness but with something of an entirely different order, with things and happenings that are threatening. We are exposed to the overwhelming force of nature, to the fury it can unleash, to the storms in which it rages. Like all animate beings, we need shelter from the elements and protection from other threatening natural forms. Whereas nature's display of beauty has the capacity to draw us beyond ourselves, to reimplace us in the ascent toward being, its turnaround serves to drive us back to our vulnerability, to our situatedness amidst things and the elements.

The advent of modern technology has opened up possibilities that, when oriented and actualized by a certain politics, have provoked a kind of return of nature that is unprecedented. Technology provides means by which nature can be rendered largely controllable and thus can be submitted to human aims, transposed into the infrastructure of the human world. At the extreme, nature suffers such destitution that it remains little more than a resource to fuel the system of market economy geared to consumption. The return that is provoked at this extreme is not one in which nature would come back to itself or in which, as itself, it would again open up to human sensibility. Rather, it returns as if from the grave, often in deadly form, like a ghost of what it once was. It returns in the form of pollutants that poison the air and water, in the ever more frequent occurrences of tornadoes, hurricanes, and other gigantic disturbances destructive of life on a vast scale, and in the form of climate change, the melting of glaciers and polar icecaps, and the chain of consequences thereof. The use of fossil fuel is only one example of the way in which the political-technological reshaping or denaturing of the total human environment produces effects that endanger the very possibility of this environment and indeed of human life itself. Even the human body becomes a site of such denaturing exchange, as the methods by which an abundance of food can be produced prove also to render many of these foods detrimental to health. It is in this situation that capitalist rhetoric adopts the cynical course of invoking nature in order to stave off the public reaction against the total industrialization of the things of everyday life: one is to purchase and consume foods that are declared to be natural even though they are often produced in quite unnatural ways and settings and in forms that have no counterpart whatsoever in nature.

Such practice is indicative of the mendaciousness that can be promoted by appeal to nature and to what is natural, by the claim that certain actions serve to restore what is natural, to return nature to itself. Such claims can serve—and indeed have, all too often, served—to conceal the wanton violence against both humanity and nature that such actions may in fact involve. Purity, uniformity, even solidarity are among the banners under which such fraudulent restorations of what is natural advance their cause.

The stakes could not be higher: in order to counter such claims and to address the denaturing effects released through a technology governed by the politics of unlimited production and consumption, the sense of nature as such must be recovered and redetermined. This task requires both retrieving antecedent senses and determinations of nature—as, for example, among the Greeks—and also thinking the sense of nature anew in a way that takes account of such distinctively modern developments as—to give a prime example—those of recent astronomy, which now reveal the expanse of the cosmos on a scale far exceeding any that could previously have been envisioned and which cannot but bring about a transformation of our conception of the place of the human. This is a task that future thinking can evade only at the greatest peril.

Both the prevalence of the cynical and empty claim to restore the natural and the ambivalence spawned by the denaturing of nature mark the retreat of nature from human sense and sensibility. The sense of nature, in every sense of *sense*, has withdrawn, and the capacity to abide with nature in a way that both exemplifies and discloses our genuine belonging to it risks being entirely lost. In the words of the American naturalist Henry Beston, who nurtured this capacity during his long, mostly solitary stay on the dunes of Cape Cod: "The world today is sick to its thin blood for lack of elemental things, for fire before the hands, for water welling from the earth, for air, for the dear earth itself underfoot." At the outermost bound where sea meets land, Beston found that "the great rhythms of nature, today so dully disregarded, wounded even, have here their spacious and primeval liberty; cloud and shadow of cloud, wind and tide, tremor of night and day."[1]

Such writers as Beston attest that, however attenuated our comportment to nature may have become, there persists some sense of nature, some experience of its appeal. Words such as those of Beston can awaken this sense, as in his account of the sounds in nature: "The three great elemental sounds in nature are the sound of rain, the sound of wind in a primeval wood, and the sound of outer ocean on a beach. I have heard them all, and of the three elemental voices, that of ocean is the most awesome, beautiful and varied." He declares that "the sea has many voices." He entreats his reader: "Listen to the surf, really lend it your ears, and you will hear in it a world of sounds"; he concludes then with a brief catalogue of the sounds that are to be heard: "hollow boomings and heavy roarings, great watery tumblings and tramplings, long hissing seethes," and so on.[2]

Yet even aside from words, even in silence, in the silence that may be prompted by the presence of elemental nature, a nascent sense of nature attunes our senses to the sight and sound of ocean waves crashing against a rocky shore. One lingers there, engaged in the sight and sound, drawn to them by an interest rooted in an elemental sense of nature. One lives in the sight and sound, not for the sake of cognition, but in order to sense—and to enhance one's sense of—nature, in a sense of sense that is antecedent to the very distinction between the sense of the senses and the sense that is construed and set apart as meaning.

The irrepressible appeal that nature retains despite its vast denaturing is attested by the efforts now made to preserve some small areas of unspoiled nature. Such wilderness areas are intended to allow the sense of nature to be revivified, although a denaturing effect analogous to that of technology threatens such areas as they become overcrowded with tourists whose presence destroys the very quality they presumably seek. In any case, such wilderness areas came to be established—indeed,

---

1. Henry Beston, *The Outermost House* (New York: Viking Press, 1928), 10, 2.
2. Ibid., 43.

the very idea of wilderness gained currency—precisely as we lost to a large degree our capacity to live with *the wild*, with an alterity in nature that cannot be controlled by the mechanics of human culture. Perhaps nothing demonstrates the wild more directly than the sudden emergence of an animal—a deer, for instance—from the woods, an appearance that can be just as unpredictable and unaccountable as the deer's slipping away, back into the cover that the woods provide. As technology becomes ever more capable, through electronic mediation, of ensuring constant presence, indeed even of what is most remote, we risk losing entirely our sense for such slipping in and out of the limits of presence.

The withdrawal of the sense of nature is replicated at the more abstract level by uncertainty about the very meaning of the word. Both the extent of its reference and the parameters that would delimit its meaning are grasped only in the vague manner requisite for any discourse whatsoever. It is this uncertainty and lack of limits that make possible the current manipulation and inflation of the designation *natural* for ends that have little to do with the preservation or restoration of what is natural. There is uncertainty as to just how far nature extends. That it includes mountains, lakes, wildlife, all the things of the earth that are not made by humans, seems somewhat assured. But it is a bit less certain whether it extends also to the earth itself and the sky, along with all that happens in and comes from the sky—rain and snow, thunder and lightning, the formation and movement of clouds. There is much greater uncertainty whether nature also extends to the other planets of the solar system, and it is still more uncertain whether the billions upon billions of other stars belong to nature. Is nature to be distinguished from the cosmos at large, or are they to be identified as one and the same? There is uncertainty, too, regarding the nature that we, sharing a great deal with other animate beings, bear in ourselves. Even the artifacts that humans produce, that, according to the ancient distinction, come about by art or craft (τέχνη) rather than by nature, consist ultimately of nothing but natural materials that have been reshaped and rearranged.

It would seem that only language and thought lie somewhat outside—or at least at the limit of—nature. For what is meant in and through a linguistic utterance is never, in principle, not just in fact, to be found among natural things. Equal sticks and stones can readily be perceived among things, but one will never find in nature equality itself as it is signified in speech. Yet, even language has its bond to nature: it is activated, it becomes actual, only in speaking or in writing. The bond of thinking to nature is more tenuous: the triangle itself (with its specific determinations) that can be an object of thought is not dependent on the visible image of it that may be sketched, though through its relation to other powers and to the human as such, even thinking is—if mediately—drawn back toward nature.

On the one hand, it seems, then, that the extension is almost unlimited, that there is little or nothing that does not somehow belong to nature. Yet, on the other hand, our sense of nature, withdrawn though it be, prompts us to resist such unlimited extension. This ambivalence is nowhere more clearly attested than in Emerson's first book, entitled simply *Nature*. At the outset Emerson introduces two distinct senses of nature, both of which are operative throughout his text. The sense that he designates as philosophical echoes the language and conceptuality of early German Idealism. Nature in this sense extends almost without limit: "all that is separate from us, all which Philosophy distinguishes as the NOT ME, that is, both nature and art, all other men and my own body, must be ranked under this name, NATURE." Yet from this sense Emerson distinguishes what he terms the common sense of nature: it "refers to essences unchanged by man; space, the air, the river, the leaf."[3]

Each of these senses of nature governs, respectively, certain passages in *Nature*. Often these passages and the sense of nature operative in them are distinct, though there are points where the two senses are brought together. The passages where such crossing of these senses occurs are especially significant.

It is primarily the common sense of nature that is operative at the outset, though already there is a gesture toward a larger sense, if not yet the philosophical sense. Emerson begins the text proper by writing of solitude and of the means that can serve our need to retire into solitude. This turn away from society and even from read or written words, this turn back to oneself, does not, however, issue in a pure relation to self; the withdrawal into solitude does not consist in recourse to an inner reflexivity in which one would intuit oneself. Rather, it is a retreat into self carried out precisely by opening oneself to certain configurations lying outside oneself, even aloof from oneself. Emerson writes: "But if a man would be alone, let him look at the stars." It is by opening oneself to nature that one returns to oneself: "The stars awaken a certain reverence, because though always present, they are inaccessible; but all natural objects make a kindred impression, when the mind is open to

---

3. Ralph Waldo Emerson, *Nature*, in *Selected Writings of Ralph Waldo Emerson*, ed. Brooks Atkinson (New York: Random House, 1940), 4. Originally published in 1836.

their influence."[4] Here it is evident that Emerson takes a path different from that represented by one, often dominant motif in early German Idealism. This motif is perhaps best expressed in the opening sentence of Fichte's *First Introduction to the Wissenschaftslehre*: "Attend to yourself: turn your vision away from all that surrounds you, and into your interiority [*in dein Inneres*]—this is the first demand that philosophy places on its student."[5] For Emerson, on the contrary, it is a certain kind of turn outward, a certain apprehension of surrounding—or even remote—nature that enables the turn inward. He writes of the lover of nature as one "whose inward and outward senses are still truly adjusted to each other."[6] The same holds for the one who would turn to himself and retire into solitude.

Yet, how is it that openness to nature serves the inward turn, the return to self? Emerson refers to "the greatest delight" that nature offers: it is the suggestion of an "occult relation" between man and nature. This relation is clearly not the common perceptual relation, nor even such relation as is established through action. How is it that when, above and beyond the common relation, nature presents itself in still another mode, when it returns in another guise, it prompts the return to self? Since the relation is an occult one, that is, a relation that is to some degree concealed, that is not immediately manifest, a certain attunement is necessary in order to hear this suggestion and to decipher what it suggests. The relation that is suggested is itself an attunement, an attunement of nature to man—such that one can declare, in Emerson's words: "I am not alone and unacknowledged."[7] Another name for this attunement is purposiveness, the purposiveness of nature with respect to man and his mental powers. The apprehension of such purposiveness issues in a kind of pleasure that is not the pleasure of sense. Emerson calls it "the greatest delight."

For Emerson nature does not consist only of natural things or material but also includes the processes, the circulation between the things

4. Ibid., 5.
5. J. G. Fichte, *Erste Einleitung in die Wissenschaftslehre*, in vol. 1 of *Werke* (Berlin: Walter de Gruyter, 1971), 422. Originally published in 1797. It must be noted that this sentence expresses only the beginning of the *Wissenschaftslehre* (as it is presented in this text). Through the systematic development of the *Wissenschaftslehre*, there is eventually a circling back to the beginning through which the very condition of the beginning is revealed.
6. Emerson, *Nature*, 6.
7. Ibid., 7.

of nature. In addition, it includes the natural elements. Though he stops short of explicitly distinguishing them from things, he enumerates the elements in almost the same manner as the early Greek philosophers would have: "this ocean of air above, this ocean of water beneath, this firmament of earth between[,] this zodiac of lights, this tent of dropping clouds, this striped coat of climates, this fourfold year."[8] He goes on to include, among other items, fire, water, and stones. In this enumeration, which contains elements pertaining to various dimensions, including time, it is still the common sense of nature that is operative; but now this sense is explicitly broadened to include the natural elements.

Emerson writes of the beauty of nature and of the love of natural beauty in a manner that displays how thoroughly he has appropriated Kant's *Critique of Judgment* and rethought its most fundamental analyses within his own systematic framework and in his own idiom. In reference to their beauty, he says "that the primary forms, as the sky, the mountain, the tree, the animal, give us a delight *in and for themselves*; a pleasure arising from outline, color, motion, and grouping."[9] He distinguishes between the simple perception of natural forms, which are restorative, and the love of the higher beauty of nature. As forms of the latter, he distinguishes between the love directed at the beauty displayed by action and that which relates to the intellect or thought. Emerson declares that the intellectual love of beauty is taste. Yet, such beauty of nature is not merely for contemplation but also comes to be re-formed in the mind so as to enable the creation of beauty. Such creation is art. Since it is from the beauty of nature that beautiful art arises, natural beauty enjoys a certain priority with respect to artistic beauty. Emerson writes: "Thus in art does Nature work through the will of a man filled with the beauty of her first works."[10] Differently expressed: it is through such a man that "nature gives the rule to art."[11] Such a man, the genuine artist, embodies the talent that Kant calls genius.

In his reflections on the beauty of nature, Emerson remains within the compass of the common sense of nature, as he does also as he goes on to trace the dependence of language on natural forms. In the most succinct formulation: "Words are signs of natural facts," and every

---

    8. Ibid., 8.
    9. Ibid., 9.
   10. Ibid., 14.
   11. Immanuel Kant, *Kritik der Urteilskraft*, in vol. 5 of *Werke: Akademie Textausgabe* (Berlin: Walter de Gruyter, 1968), §46. Originally published in 1790.

word, "if traced to its root, is found to be borrowed from some material appearance."[12] He offers numerous examples of such dependence on natural forms: that *transgression* means—that is, is derived from—the crossing of a line; and that *spirit* primarily means wind. It is the heart that expresses emotion, and the head that denotes thought. All these natural forms, those that shine forth in their beauty and those from which language—even if in a way that exceeds nature—nonetheless arises, belong to nature in its common sense.

Yet, throughout much of Emerson's text there are junctures where the philosophical sense of nature is broached. Even as he celebrates the delight born of the suggestion of an occult relation between man and nature, alluding to the purposiveness of natural forms, he declares that "Nature always wears the colors of the spirit." Or, again, amidst his discussion of language, he writes that "Nature is the symbol of spirit." Or, still more succinctly: "behind nature, throughout nature, spirit is present." Furthermore, this bond is to be respected and replicated on the side of the human: one "cannot be a naturalist until he satisfies all the demands of the spirit."[13]

It is, then, by way of the concept of spirit that Emerson weaves into his text the philosophical sense of nature. If nature is determined as the *not-me*, then spirit is what lies on the side of the *me*, of the self; yet, it is by no means identical with the individual self but is rather that which is indwelling in—that which animates—all selves, thereby constituting them as selves and as higher-order communities. In the later parts of Emerson's text, the philosophical sense of nature becomes dominant, especially in the sections aptly entitled "Spirit" and "Idealism." Here Emerson's writing attests to his thorough appropriation of the absolute idealism of Schelling and Hegel—as in this remarkable passage: "There seems to be a necessity in spirit to manifest itself in material forms; and day and night, river and storm, beast and bird, acid and alkali, preexist in necessary Ideas in the mind of God, and are what they are by virtue of preceding affections in the world of spirit."[14]

There is no other passage in which the crossing of the two senses of nature, indeed their integration, is manifest to the same degree. The natural forms that Emerson enumerates are things and elements exemplifying the common sense of nature; and yet, these are installed within

---

12. Emerson, *Nature*, 14.
13. Ibid., 7, 14, 35, 41.
14. Ibid., 19.

the compass of the manifestation of spirit in nature, and thus within the framework of the philosophical sense of nature as determined by its relation to spirit. It is in nature, in just such things and elements as Emerson enumerates, that spirit becomes manifest.

This passage is also most transparently a reinscription of the idealistic triad that constitutes the principal moments in the systematic development: the idea ("God as he is in his eternal essence before the creation of nature and finite spirit"[15]); nature ("the idea in the form of otherness"[16]); and spirit ("the transition from nature to spirit ... is only a coming-to-itself of spirit out of its self-externality in nature"[17]).

The most decisive feature of this configuration as it is described by Emerson is the mutual dependence of spirit and nature. On the one hand, nature is dependent on, even subordinated to, spirit; it is merely that in which spirit manifests itself. Especially in those places where Emerson's discourse is largely governed by the philosophical sense of nature, the stress falls on the subordination of nature; thus he writes of being led "to regard nature as phenomenon, not a substance; to attribute necessary existence to spirit; to esteem nature as an accident and an effect."[18] He refers also to the manner in which culture has the effect of "degrading nature and suggesting its dependence on spirit."[19] Yet, on the other hand, nature is by no means dispensable for spirit; rather, it is necessary in order that spirit be able to manifest itself: insofar as spirit is determined as the movement of manifestation of itself to itself, its very constitution as spirit is dependent on nature. Without nature there could be no spirit. Mutual dependence of nature and spirit is, it seems, hinted at by the texture of Emerson's writing about the self-manifestation of spirit, by the way in which he inserts into the description of the philosophical configuration the designations of various particular natural forms such as day and night, river and storm.

According to Emerson, nature is at the root of language even as our words are elevated to the highest spiritual level. Furthermore, when

---

15. G. W. F. Hegel, *Wissenschaft der Logik*, Erster Teil, in vol. 21 of *Gesammelte Werke* (Hamburg: Felix Meiner, 1985), 34. Dated 1832. Emerson writes that the "aptitude for metaphysical inquiries ... fastens the attention upon immortal necessary uncreated natures, that is, upon Ideas" (*Nature*, 31).
16. Hegel, *Enzyklopädie der philosophischen Wissenschaften (1830)* (Frankfurt a.M.: Suhrkamp, 1970), §247.
17. Hegel, *Enzyklopädie*, §381 *Zusatz*.
18. Emerson, *Nature*, 27.
19. Ibid., 32.

language is raised to this level and addressed to spirit as such, its reach proves insufficient, and its failure prompts a certain recourse to nature. In one of the most incisive passages in *Nature*, Emerson writes: "Of that ineffable essence which we call Spirit, he that thinks most, will say least." Words suited to spirit are lacking. The words that we address to it fail to disclose it; they recoil back upon us and teach us silence. One who has learned silence, who says least because he thinks most, engages instead a kind of vision, a foresight. Emerson continues: "We can foresee God in the coarse, and, as it were, distant phenomena of matter; but when we try to define and describe himself, both language and thought desert us, and we are as helpless as fools and savages." God, the idea, which is actualized in and as spirit, yields neither to language nor to thought. Our words fail to such an extent that they no more touch spirit than does the babbling of fools or the unintelligible utterances of savages. If one who speaks least does so because he has thought most, it is not because his thought has succeeded in reaching and disclosing spirit but rather because he has carried his thinking through to the point where it recoils on itself and its failure is revealed. Emerson again stresses the incapacity of language but then continues by describing how, in the face of this incapacity, there is necessarily recourse to nature and to the foresight that nature makes possible. In his words: "That essence refuses to be recorded in propositions, but when man has worshipped him intellectually, the noblest ministry of nature is to stand as the apparition of God. It is the organ through which the universal spirit speaks to the individual, and strives to lead back the individual to it."[20] It is in view of this recourse to nature that Emerson writes: "Therefore is Nature ever the ally of Religion."[21]

The mutual dependence of spirit and nature is, at most, expounded as such in only a few passages in Emerson's text. Most passages relevant to the description of this dependence fall on one side or the other, portraying either spirit or nature as primary and the other as dependent. As a result there is a hiatus that, rather than occurring at a particular juncture, extends throughout the text; that is, there emerges an ambivalence and, in particular, an ambivalence regarding nature. On the one side, nature is reduced, rendered subordinate to spirit; it is taken to be only the phenomenal, accidental appearance of spirit. Through the self-recognition of spirit in nature, nature would be thoroughly appropriated

20. Ibid., 34.
21. Ibid., 23.

to spirit. On the other side, nature would be deemed indispensable to spirit. It would be acknowledged as the site to which recourse would necessarily be had in order that human foresight—and to this extent manifestation—of spirit could take place. This ambivalence reproduces in inverse form the ambivalence mentioned earlier between the unlimited extension of nature and the resistance to such extension that is prompted by our residual sense of nature.

The ambivalence regarding the relation of dependence between spirit and nature is, in turn, compounded. On each side there are two quite different directions in which the determination of nature can be carried out. The subordination of nature to spirit may be developed in the direction of the distinctly human spirit in such a way that nature is regarded as submitting to human aims. In one of his most revealing statements in this direction, Emerson writes: "Nature is thoroughly mediate. It is made to serve. It receives the dominion of man as meekly as the ass on which the Saviour rode. It offers all its kingdoms to man as the raw material which he may mould into what is useful. . . . One after another his victorious thought comes up with and reduces all things, until the world becomes at last only a realized will—the double of the man."[22]

Here one side of the ambivalence, that of the dependence or subordination of nature, is developed in a direction that itself splits into two ways in which nature can be determined. This side of the ambivalence thus itself produces a further ambivalence. In this development both spirit and nature are stripped of their theological and dialectical import, or, at least, within the compass of this development such import is bracketed. Then, with this reorientation to the merely human spirit, Emerson in effect declares, on the one hand, the reduction of nature to mere raw material for human enterprise and, on the other hand, the transformation of nature into the site of the realization of the human will. His conception of the subordination of nature thus comes to vacillate between the basic postulate of a certain technology and the practical postulate of the identity of man and nature as the goal of human striving.

On the other side of the ambivalence, that of the dependence of spirit on nature, there is also a development in a certain direction, namely, toward determination of nature as the site of manifestation. This development also splits into two ways, producing a further

22. Ibid., 22.

ambivalence. On the one hand, nature is determined as the apparition of God, of spirit, as such; it is that in and through which, once language and thought fail, our foresight can envision spirit. Whereas this determination is governed by the philosophical sense of nature, there is, on the other hand, a determination much closer to the common sense. In it nature is regarded as that which offers us the greatest delight through its suggestion of its hidden accord with man. It is this other determination that is operative when, by looking at the stars, we are led back to ourselves and enabled to enter into solitude.

On both sides of the ambivalence, there is a return of nature to spirit. On the one side, the space between nature and spirit is effectively closed, and the difference separating them, their twofoldness, is abolished. Either nature is reduced to raw material to be integrated into human enterprise and hence abolished as nature; or its total assimilation to spirit is posited as the aim of human endeavor. On the other side, nature returns to spirit, but in a manner that preserves their difference, their twofoldness. Either nature is the site required for spirit's manifestation as such, or else nature, in particular forms, is that to which we open ourselves in order that we might retreat into ourselves, into solitude. On this other side, which preserves the otherness of nature, nature returns to spirit, not by way of assimilation, but in such a way that spirit shines through nature drawn toward it, through proximate nature. By offering the site where spirit can manifest itself, nature lets spirit be itself and lets us return to ourselves.

Emerson's exposure of the proliferating ambivalences regarding nature in its relation to spirit is set against the background of modern philosophy, especially that of German Idealism. Through his exposition Emerson brings out the various ways in which nature returns to spirit, ways that for the most part are expounded in a more limited way by his predecessors and not in the full configuration. Rousseau, Thoreau, and in a certain moment of his thought even Kant[23] call for a return to nature that would let nature return to the domain, indeed to the self-understanding, of humans. Although they conceive this return in quite different ways, they concur entirely in considering this return of nature to be such that nature is not simply assimilated to spirit. Each would endorse, if in different manners, Emerson's portrayal of one who

---

23. This moment is found in the *Critique of Judgment* (§42) at the point where Kant expounds on the superiority of natural beauty over artistic beauty. See my discussion below in chap. 2.

by looking at the stars—or perhaps at other natural things or configurations—is enabled to retreat into solitude.

Marx is situated on the opposite side, for which spirit, conceived as human society under various material conditions, has absolute priority over nature such that nature, reduced to the matter that is employed and also transformed by industry, would be assimilated to what would otherwise be called spirit. In his critique of Feuerbach's conception of the sensible world as object of contemplation and feeling, Marx maintains that this world is merely the product of industry and the state of society. Regarding that portion of nature that has not yet been subjected to human mastery, Marx writes: "But with every new invention, with each step forward by industry, a new piece of the terrain will be broken off, and the basis from which the examples for similar Feuerbachean propositions arise thus becomes smaller."[24]

And yet, today one can no longer overlook the fact that the steps forward by industry by which further pieces of the natural terrain are progressively broken off—that is, assimilated—has provoked a return of nature in deadly, ghostly forms that threaten life at all levels. The example of pollutants from communist eastern Europe (right up to the time of the system's collapse), threatening life and contaminating natural elements such as air and water on which life depends, is perhaps the strongest evidence against the Marxist reduction of nature. The return of nature in such deadly form can no longer be ignored when pollutants from eastern Europe spread so far that they kill trees in the Black Forest. Yet, this deadly return of nature, if among the most extreme, is by no means unique. Today there are few places on earth that are immune to such return.

Such an unabashed declaration of the reduction of nature as put forth by Marx is not to be found in Hegel. Rather, for Hegel there remains ambivalence not only in the primary articulations of his system as elaborated in the *Encyclopedia* but also in various other dimensions. Specifically, the ambivalence concerns the standing of nature, whether nature is assimilated to spirit, and if not, then whether it is, in any sense, submitted to something other. Both the play of ambivalence and the assertion of nature's detachment from spirit can be discerned perhaps most distinctly in Hegel's earliest published texts.

---

24. Karl Marx, *Die Deutsche Ideologie*, in vol. 2 of *Frühe Schriften*, ed. Hans-Joachim Lieber and Peter Furth (Darmstadt: Wissenschaftliche Buchgesellschaft, 1975), 53. Written in 1845–46 in collaboration with Engels; first published in 1932.

In the Preface to the *Differenzschrift* (as it is commonly designated), Hegel identifies the principle of speculation: "The principle of speculation is the identity of subject and object."[25] Hegel formulates this principle in the course of his critical appraisal of Kant's accomplishment: Kant indeed establishes the identity of subject and object, but only within the limits of the categories. For the categories (Hegel eliminates those of modality) express acts of thought that constitute—and in content are identical with—the *a priori* determinations of objects, whereas all further determinations remain *a posteriori*. While Fichte advances beyond these limits, eliminating the vast *a posteriori* realm that remains for Kant, the opposition is recast, since the identity of subject and object, of the I and the not-I, becomes the goal of an infinite striving.[26] The identity of subject and object, of spirit and nature, continues to be established only on the side of the subject; it remains a subjective subject-object.[27] The genuine advance—which Hegel endorses—beyond this position is carried out by Schelling: "in the philosophy of nature Schelling sets the objective subject-object beside the subjective subject-object and presents both as united in something higher than the subject."[28] This move is anything but an assimilation of the object to the subject, of nature to spirit; it is rather an advance beyond the position of transcendental philosophy, which grants dominant status to the subject. In this way Schelling satisfies "the need for a philosophy that will

---

25. Hegel, *Differenz des Fichte'schen und Schelling'schen Systems der Philosophie*, in vol. 4 of *Gesammelte Werke* (Hamburg: Felix Meiner, 1968), 6. Originally published in 1801. This principle is echoed in Emerson's *Nature*, though in a more concretely immediate form and in Emerson's own idiom, when he writes of the inward and outward senses being truly adjusted to each other (Emerson, *Nature*, 6).

26. Since Emerson identifies nature in the philosophical sense with the not-I, his conception of nature as "only a realized will, the double of the man" (*Nature*, 22) is closely allied to that of Fichte; for Emerson, however, this conception is merely one moment within the configuration of ambivalences.

27. The limitation in Fichte's system to a subjective subject-object is also evident in the deductive oscillation between idealism and realism, which finally converges on the check or impulse (*Anstoss*) that initiates the self-limitation by which the I posits the not-I or object over against itself. This mere check on the I's activity is, as it were, the sole trace that remains of the object, which in every other respect is assimilated to the I or subject. See Hegel, *Differenz*, 48; also Fichte, *Grundlage der gesammten Wissenschaftslehre*, in vol. 1 of *Werke*, 210; also my discussion in *Spacings—of Reason and Imagination in Texts of Kant, Fichte, Hegel* (Chicago: University of Chicago Press, 1987), 63.

28. Hegel, *Differenz*, 7.

recompense nature for the mishandling that it suffered in Kant's and Fichte's systems."²⁹

In his comparison of Schelling's philosophy with Fichte's, which constitutes the third major part of the *Differenzschrift*, Hegel explains how nature is recompensed in Schelling's system. He reiterates his criticism of Fichte's system: that it is limited in that it recognizes only a subjective subject-object. Again Hegel focuses on the advance that Schelling makes beyond this limitation: to the subjective subject-object an objective subject-object is added. These are, in turn, to be united in something higher—or, as Hegel now expresses it: "so that the absolute presents itself in each of the two subject-objects and finds itself perfected only in both together as the highest synthesis."³⁰ Granted that the task of philosophy is the suspension of dichotomy (*die Aufhebung der Entzweiung*), Hegel rejects the attempt to achieve this by nullifying (*vernichten*) one of the opposites and exalting the other, for such a would-be solution leaves the opposition intact. Instead, it is necessary that both subject and object be sublated or suspended (*aufgehoben*) as subject and object and be posited as identical. Yet, as he writes: "In the absolute identity subject and object are sublated, but because they are within the absolute identity they both have standing too." Or again: "Philosophy must give the separation into subject and object its due. . . . Hence, the absolute itself is the identity of identity and non-identity; being opposed and being one are both together in it."³¹ In its very identity with the subject (both as subject-object), the object sustains nonetheless its separation from the subject. Nature, in its very identity with spirit, remains nonetheless separate from spirit. It is, most decidedly, not assimilated to spirit.

Such relationality Hegel expresses in the speculative word *Aufheben* (to sublate or suspend). The word is speculative because it has two opposed meanings. On the one side, it means to preserve (*aufbewahren*), to maintain (*erhalten*). On the other side, it means to let cease (*aufhören lassen*), to put an end to (*ein Ende machen*). When something involved in such relationality ceases, comes to an end, it is not simply annihilated (*vernichtet*) but only loses its immediacy and enters into unity with its opposite.³² Thus, to say that nature is sublated (*aufgehoben*) is not to say that it is nullified, as it would be if assimilated to spirit, but rather that

---

29. Ibid., 8.
30. Ibid., 63.
31. Ibid., 63f.
32. Hegel, *Wissenschaft der Logik*, 94f.

it is preserved, not as independent and immediate, but in unity with spirit—that is, as an objective subject-object. It is preserved in its difference from the very opposite with which it enters into unity. In the identity of subject and object—conceived speculatively, that is, according to what is said in the word *Aufheben*—both subject and object are preserved, but as moments that remain differentiated even as they are unified, typically in a higher unity.

It is precisely such unity of opposites preserved in their difference that Schelling expresses in his *Ideas for a Philosophy of Nature* when he writes: "Nature shall be visible spirit, and spirit invisible nature."[33] It is because of this unity—because, in Hegel's terms, each is a subject-object—that nature can provide a site for the manifestation of spirit. Yet, because one is visible (spirit) and the other invisible (nature), because, in Hegel's terms, one is objective (subject-object) and the other subjective (subject-object), their difference is preserved, and neither can be simply assimilated to the other. Though nature is brought, in differentiated unity with its opposite, under the higher unity designated as the absolute and, in the manner prescribed by the word *Aufheben*, is submitted to this higher unity, its differentiation from spirit—even if within this unity—prevents its assimilation to spirit.

In the more complex relationality of the *Encyclopedia* (1830 version), the preservation of nature from assimilation to spirit is less evident; or, in a more problematic formulation, there appears to be in Hegel's text a fault line, a trace of fissure or rift, or at least tension, between a sublation of nature and a nullifying of nature. In other words, there emerges an ambivalence regarding these two ways of conceiving the return of nature to spirit.

At the beginning of the *Philosophy of Nature*, Hegel determines nature as "the idea in the form of otherness." Yet, nature is not merely external in relation to the idea and to spirit; rather, "externality constitutes the determination in which it is as nature."[34] It occurs first in its immediate externality as space, in which the parts are purely external to one another and which, because as immediate it contains no difference within itself, is continuous. Thus, it is with space that the *Philosophy of Nature* begins.

---

33. F. W. J. Schelling, *Ideen zu einer Philosophie der Natur als Einleitung in das Studium dieser Wissenschaft*, in *Schriften von 1794–1798* (Darmstadt: Wissenschaftliche Buchgesellschaft, 1967), 380. Originally published in 1797.

34. Hegel, *Naturphilosophie*, Part 2 of *Enzyklopädie*, §247.

Following the general determination of nature, the further explanation offered is that the idea posits this other, namely, nature, outside itself "and takes it back again into itself in order to be subjectivity and spirit."[35] In other words, there is a taking up again "of this outer into the inner, an inwardizing/remembering [*Erinnern*]."[36] In still different terms, nature, posited outside the idea, is brought back into the idea, which thereby becomes spirit. Hegel writes that spirit "is the truth and the final goal of nature and the true actuality of the idea."[37] In nature as a posited moment within the unity of the idea, the content of the latter "is manifested." In other words, nature is the site of the manifestation of the idea, which through this manifestation becomes spirit. The question is whether, in manifesting the idea and being brought back into the

---

35. Ibid., §247 *Zusatz*. It is important to note that the *Zusätze* do not come directly from Hegel. For the *Philosophy of Nature*, they were put together by Hegel's student Karl Ludwig Michelet. They were compiled from written material connected with eight lecture courses on this subject over the period from 1805–6 to 1830. Some of this written material came from Hegel's lecture notes; other material came from student *Nachschriften* taken down by Michelet and three other students. A similar method for compiling the *Zusätze* was employed by Ludwig Boumann, the editor of the *Philosophy of Spirit*. This method has more recently come under serious criticism, especially in that it conflates material from very different periods and thus completely obscures the development of Hegel's thought (see the Introduction to the *Enzyklopädie*, ed. Friedhelm Nicolin and Otto Pöggeler [Hamburg: Felix Meiner, 1959], xlv–vi). Nonetheless there is considerable agreement that the *Zusätze* are indispensable to an interpretation of Hegel's thought (see J. N. Findlay's foreword to the *Philosophy of Spirit* [Oxford: Oxford University Press, 1971], v–vi). Still, a certain tentativeness is required in view of the state of these texts.

The publication of various *Nachschriften*, edited under the auspices of the Hegel Archiv in Bochum, alleviates to some degree the problems resulting from the editorial practices of Hegel's students. For example, in the *Nachschrift* of Hegel's *Lectures on the Philosophy of Spirit* from 1827/28 recorded by J. E. Erdmann and Ferdinand Walter, Hegel introduces consideration of the relation between spirit and nature by locating each, as it were, in the human. The *Nachschrift* reads: "The finite spirit stands between two worlds, one, on the side of nature, is the bodily, and separated from it, on the other side, is the infinite, the absolute" (*Vorlesungen über die Philosophie des Geistes. Berlin 1827/1828* [Hamburg: Felix Meiner, 1994], 5). Another significant example is found in the *Nachschrift* of Hegel's *Lectures on the Philosophy of Nature* from 1819/20 recorded by J. R. Ringier. Hegel says: "nature is not only the selfless, but also is being for-itself. It is just as much a matter of spirit as of the unspiritual; it is opposed to spirit but not foreign to it; rather, in this other it possesses itself" (*Vorlesungen über die Philosophie der Natur. Berlin 1819/20* [Hamburg: Felix Meiner, 2001], 5).

36. Hegel, *Enzyklopädie*, §251 *Zusatz*.
37. Ibid., §251.

idea, nature maintains a certain separation, a difference, or whether it is assimilated.

This question is more directly addressed in the introduction to the *Philosophy of Spirit*. There are several passages that appear to declare that nature is assimilated to spirit. Hegel writes that "spirit has for its presupposition nature, of which it is the truth and to which it is absolutely prior [*absolut Erstes*]. In this truth nature has vanished [*ist die Natur verschwunden*] and spirit has resulted as the idea that has reached its being-for-itself."[38] In short, the return of nature to the idea become spirit brings about the vanishing, the disappearing, the nullifying of nature, its utter assimilation to spirit. This passage is amplified in an accompanying *Zusatz*, which at a certain point reads: "Every activity of spirit is nothing but a way of reducing [*Zurückführung*] the external to the internal, which is spirit itself, and it is only by this reduction, by this idealization or assimilation [*Assimilation*] of the external, that it becomes and is spirit."[39] Taking the two passages together, it can be said that the return of nature to the idea or spirit is a reduction or assimilation of nature to spirit and that its result is to make nature vanish.

And yet, there are other passages in this very *Zusatz* that point to another way of conceiving the return of nature. The text declares that the concept or idea achieves actuality only through "the complete overcoming [*Überwindung*] of externality. . . . This first occurs in spirit, which precisely by achieving this overcoming distinguishes itself from nature."[40] The text adds that this overcoming is a "sublation of externality." It can be said, then, that this overcoming of nature by spirit does not nullify nature, for through this overcoming, spirit *distinguishes itself from nature*, which must, then, be accorded a certain standing as the condition of this distinguishing. This conclusion is confirmed by the identification of this overcoming as a sublation, for in being sublated, nature comes to be united with its opposite, with the idea, which nature is in the form of otherness; yet, though the immediate opposition is surpassed, the moments retain their distinctness, their difference. Nature is neither reduced nor assimilated to the idea or spirit.

One other passage in this *Zusatz* expresses the same conclusion. The passage reads: "the transition from nature to spirit is not a transition to something thoroughly other, but rather only a coming-to-itself

---

38. Hegel, *Philosophie des Geistes*, Part 3 of *Enzyklopädie*, §381.
39. Ibid., §381 *Zusatz*.
40. Ibid.

of spirit, which exists outside of itself in nature. But just as little is the determinate difference between nature and spirit sublated through this transition."[41] That the determinate difference is not sublated can here be taken as saying that in the return of nature to spirit, the determinate difference between nature and spirit is not cancelled, not done away with, even though nature proves identical with spirit in that it is just spirit existing outside itself.[42] By the retention of its difference from spirit, nature retains its separation, its non-assimilation, its irreducibility to spirit. Thus, taking all these passages together, it can be said that the text is ambivalent as regards the question of the return of nature.

A similar ambivalence is to be found in Hegel's *Aesthetics*, though in this text it goes almost entirely unmarked as such. The topic of these lectures (edited four years after Hegel's death by H. G. Hotho) is the philosophy of beautiful or fine art (*schöne Kunst*). This phrase indicates that the lectures do not deal with the other locus in which beauty appears, that they do not deal with the beauty of nature. Hegel emphasizes that this exclusion is not arbitrary, that it is not simply a matter of the right of a science to delimit its own subject matter. Rather, this exclusion is based on the thesis enunciated by Hegel at the outset of the lectures: "that the beauty of art is higher than nature."[43] In other words: "the work of art stands higher than any natural product."[44] It is elevated above nature because art is born of the spirit, because it is intrinsically spiritual; and, in the words of the *Aesthetics*, "everything spiritual is better than any product of nature."[45] The superiority of artistic beauty is not merely relative in comparison with nature, not merely a matter of degree. Everything beautiful is truly beautiful only by belonging to the higher sphere of spirit. The beauty of nature is no more than a pale reflection of the beauty born of the spirit, the beauty of art.

In the realm of beauty, it is not, then, a question of the assimilation of nature to spirit, of whether in its return to spirit it also retains a standing apart from spirit. Rather, in this realm it is a matter of rigorously separating nature from spirit, of setting everything natural apart from

---

41. Ibid.
42. Here it is imperative to note that the determinate difference between nature and spirit is not sublated—that is, it is not cancelled—but rather, as determinate, is the result of a sublation. In this case the word *Aufheben* is used in a non-speculative way.
43. Hegel, *Ästhetik*, ed. F. Bassenge (West Berlin: das europäische buch, 1985), 1:14. This text is based on Hotho's second edition (1842).
44. Ibid., 40.
45. Ibid.

the beautiful, spiritual work of art. Nature is degraded, not by being nullified through assimilation to spirit, but rather by being set apart as wholly inferior. Nature would return only to itself in its degraded status, its beauty merely imaging from afar the beauty of art.

Thus, everything natural would be banished from art and from its birth from spirit. And yet, there are two ways in which, despite all the exclusions, nature reenters artistic creation; acknowledgment of these returns of nature has the effect of limiting Hegel's thesis that art is born purely of the spirit. Both of these ways are indicated in Hegel's text, though their implications for the broader conception of art and nature go unmentioned.

The first of these ways is broached by the role ascribed to genius in the creation of works of art. According to Hegel's text, the productive activity of imagination (*Phantasie*) by which the artist gives external form to the rational or spiritual in the work of art is based on what is called genius and talent. Talent is the lesser of these capabilities, so much so that Hegel says that talent without genius does not go far beyond a mere external skill. Both genius and talent are, in a sense, innate; they represent "a *specific* aptitude in which a natural element plays an essential part."[46] This element is something that the subject cannot generate in himself but "must find in himself as immediately given."[47] Genius is, then, something naturally given; it is, in Kant's phrase, a "natural gift" (*Naturgabe*). Thus, having rigorously differentiated art from nature, having even required of art a certain purification from the merely natural, Hegel here grants a certain *return of nature* at the very heart of artistic creation.

There is a second way by which nature reenters artistic creation. Hegel says that the condition in the artist constituted by the activities of imagination and technical execution is what is called inspiration (*Begeisterung*). How, then, in a particular instance, does the artist become inspired? According to Hegel, this happens when, with his natural genius, the artist enters into relation with an available (*vorgefundene*) given material (*gegebende Stoff*) and finds himself solicited (*aufgefordert*) to give form to this material. Thus, inspiration requires the natural gift of genius, orientation to a particular given material, and a solicitation to artistic production stemming from that material. Indeed, says Hegel, the artist must immerse himself so thoroughly in the material that he

---

46. Ibid., 278.
47. Ibid.

forgets his own personality and is only "the form for the formation of the theme that has taken hold of him."[48] Hegel mentions the example of Shakespeare, whose material consisted of old tales, chronicles, and so forth; but rather than citing examples where the mediation of language is already thoroughly involved, it is even more to the point to mention the sculptor solicited by the marble to free, as Michelangelo attested, the forms already slumbering there.

Here, then, in the artist's being solicited and utterly absorbed in the natural material, even to the point of self-forgetting, there is a second way in which nature returns to the very heart of artistic creation. By exposing these returns of nature, Hegel shows that the rigorous separation of art and spirit from nature cannot be sustained. Nature returns, and the separation that would degrade nature is violated, even as, elsewhere in Hegel's text, it is also affirmed. The relation between nature and spirit and the form assumed by the return of nature remain ambivalent.

---

48. Ibid., 282.

2 THE BIRTH OF NATURE

Nature both exceeds and yet is bound to natural things. They, in turn, are natural in that they are by nature. Either they are, of their own accord and from an irrecoverable past, already there with the earth itself; or they come forth from within nature as the progeny of natural beings without being brought forth by human artifice. Even the things produced through human endeavor come indirectly from nature; for they require material derived from natural things, and they are produced by living beings who are by nature, even if it is a nature overlaid with conventions, practices, and forms of order that are not self-evidently by nature.

Birth occurs when from natural beings progeny that are by nature come forth within nature. To this extent nature governs their birth, determines them as natural beings, and in this way extends beyond them, exceeds them. The bonds between birth and nature are both direct yet also intertwined. Birth belongs manifoldly to nature.

Considered etymologically, the designation *birth of nature* is covertly tautological. *Nature* stems from the Latin *natura*, which by way of the participle *natus* is derived from *nascor, to be born*. The English *natal* and *natality* also stem from *nascor*; these etymologies thus connect—to the limited extent possible in this way—nature and natality, nature and birth. *Natura* is the translation of the Greek φύσις, which displays the same connection with birth. It derives from φύω, which means *to bring forth, to beget*, and which in the passive-middle form φύομαι means *to come forth, to be begotten*, or *born*. These etymological affinities indicate that the ancients spoke—and could not but have spoken—of nature and birth as intrinsically connected and thereby were prompted to think them together.

Although in modern European languages the connection is less apparent, it can be disclosed through phenomenally oriented reflection: nature is the place where birth takes place. It is in nature, even if in a nature that has been reshaped by human endeavor, that one finds oneself having been born. In the recognition of natality, there comes about an awareness that one must always, since birth, have been exposed to the sunlight, the wind, the rain, the darkness of night—that is, to elemental nature. Furthermore, in having been born in a certain place, one has been born into a particular linguistic context, usually that of a single language, and in most cases a trace of that linguistic context will be borne in one's voice. One will also have been born into a variety of more or less definite views and beliefs (what the Greeks called δόξα), and even if later these may be submitted to criticism, they constitute a point of departure to which a certain affiliation—even if critical—is likely to remain.

Yet, in finding oneself as having been born, one cannot recapture one's own birth; there is—as one can indeed become aware—an indefinite but insuperable limit beyond which one cannot recover oneself, a limit beyond which memory has no power whatsoever. The event of one's own birth is secured from all reflective intrusion. It is as if, in Schelling's phrase, there were a kind of "life before this life,"[1] a life, a bestowal of the gift of life, irrecoverable in the afterlife that is securely one's own. Submission to natality involves not only birth, the necessity of being born, but also finding oneself as having been born in a past that was never present.

Nature is a place. It is the place from within which natural things are born and determined as such. It is a place to which all living beings are, in some manner or other, drawn back. It is a place that extends beneath even the most thoroughly fabricated centers of human endeavor. It is the place within which lies the locale to which, in having been born there, one is bound, even if by bonds that can be loosened, attenuated, and after some time virtually broken. Such place has only the most tenuous relation to the homogeneous space conceived through abstraction from all the things of nature. Rather, it is both a place replete with things and a place the very constitution of which is determined by the reception offered to all that takes place within it and to all things that

---

1. F. W. J. Schelling, *Philosophische Untersuchungen über das Wesen der menschlichen Freiheit*, in *Ausgewählte Werke, Schriften von 1806–1813* (Darmstadt: Wissenschaftliche Buchgesellschaft, 1968), 331.

take their place within it. These things are for the most part born, even if most lack the reflexivity that would allow them to turn back toward their birth. Some come forth from the earth, emerging into the light; some are born directly or indirectly from others of their kind. These births and all that comes in their train are supported by the earth and by all that in which the earth appears in another guise, by stones, soil, mountains. The character of these tends to coalesce with that of the elements such as rain, wind, snow, forests, and indeed the earth itself. The earth is the receptacle of nature and, as bounded by the sky, provides the place where life can come forth, where new life, a life that previously was not (though it may, later, seem to itself to have been), even a life that is a self still to come, can come to be through a birth that will ever remain withdrawn from this life. Encompassed and supported by the earth, nature is the place of birth, the mother of all things (in a sense that is not at all merely metaphorical). The genitive is, first of all, subjective, and the phrase *birth of nature* refers to birth as belonging to nature.

Among the ancients there persisted a basic orientation to φύσις—hence to nature and birth. Among the early Greek thinkers from the Milesians to Empedocles, this orientation was all-determining; with only the slightest hyperbole, one could say that these thinkers thought nothing but φύσις, that all things on which their thought focused were brought back finally to φύσις as their ἀρχή, as that from which they were born. Empedocles, to take a prime example, thought the ἀρχή as consisting neither of elements (στοιχεῖα) nor of being (τὸ ὄν), but rather as roots (ῥιζώματα), as that from which certain living things originate and by which they are nourished and sustained. Here there is, in particular, no reference whatsoever to making or production (ποίησις) as in the imposition of form on more or less shapeless material.

It is with Plato that the paradigm of production begins to play a prominent role. The structure of production is more precisely articulated: in making something, an artisan looks to a model and forms his product in such a way that it looks like—has the look of—the model. In the *Timaeus* the god who makes the cosmos is called a δημιουργός, an artisan or craftsman, and also simply a maker (ποιητής). And yet, the god is also called father (πατήρ). This double naming introduces into the account the opposition between ποίησις and φύσις, between production and birth/nature. In the second of Timaeus' major discourses, the paradigm of birth—of begetting, giving birth, being born—becomes dominant. This is perhaps most explicit in Timaeus' description of the three kinds: "At present it is necessary to think of three kinds: that which comes to be, that in which it comes to be, and that from which that which comes to be is copied and begotten [φύεται]. And furthermore, it is fitting to liken the receiver to a mother, the *from which* to a father, and the nature [φύσιν, i.e., φύσις] between these to an offspring."[2] The threefold posited in this passage stands in marked contrast to the twofold of model and product that defines production. Yet not only does this passage describe the three kinds and bring to their description the paradigm of birth or procreation, but also, by its way of including the word φύσις, it indicates that the third of the three kinds, the offspring that is born, is nature and all that is by nature.

While with Plato the two paradigms are operative side by side, often in a certain tension, subsequently that of production becomes dominant and with only few exceptions runs surreptitiously throughout the course of Western philosophy; it is sustained by such oppositions as that of form and matter (or content). It is only with Schelling that this paradigm is for the most part set aside and that of nature and birth reinstated at the center of philosophical thought. Indeed, Schelling regards this turn to nature, which lets nature return to the prominence it had with the early Greek thinkers, as what, perhaps most of all, sets his thought apart from the entire course followed by modern philosophy. This contrast is most evident in Schelling's charge: "All modern European philosophy since its beginning (with Descartes) has this common defect [or lack—*Mangel*], that nature does not exist for it and that it lacks a living ground."[3]

In the form of transcendental idealism, Kant and Fichte bring the philosophy of the subject to its highest point; and yet, it is precisely in these figures that the alleged defect of modern philosophy becomes evident. This is demonstrated both in Hegel's critical approach to Fichte in the *Differenzschrift* (1801) and in Schelling's insistence, in the *System of Transcendental Idealism* (1800), that transcendental philosophy must have as its counterpart a philosophy of nature. Yet, though a certain ambivalence remains, the development of Hegel's thought displays a tendency to affirm the dominance of spirit over nature, or at least to require that there be an *Aufhebung* through which the opposition between spirit and nature is resolved by their being raised into the higher unity of the absolute. Initially Schelling embraced the system of absolute idealism or

---

2. Plato, *Timaeus* 50c–d.
3. Schelling, *Über das Wesen der menschlichen Freiheit*, 300.

absolute identity that resulted.[4] But in *On the Essence of Human Freedom* (1809), he introduces at the heart of his system a withdrawal of nature from spirit, a return of nature in which it returns to itself.

Beginning with the debate over pantheism that had been provoked by the reception of Spinoza, Schelling undertakes to develop a system of grounding; that is, he sets out to display the structure by which the totality of things is grounded on its ground. It is a system that can be regarded as fundamentally ethical in that it takes up the questions of freedom and of good and evil. It can also be considered theological, for it develops an account of the nature of God, even though of a God whose relation to nature renders him quite otherwise than he is conceived in Western philosophy and theology. Yet, what underlies and makes possible both the ethical and the theological conceptions is the fundamentally new ontology that Schelling develops. This priority of the ontological is corroborated by the *Stuttgart Private Lectures*, given only one year after the publication of *On the Essence of Human Freedom*. There Schelling says: "Thus the two principles in God are related as a being [or: that which is—*Seyendes*] and being [*Seyn*]."[5] He distinguishes, then, between the God that is (*der seyende Gott*) and the being of God (*das Sein des Gottes*).

The ontological task is, then, to determine the grounding structure. Throughout much of the history of philosophy the name for the ground of all beings is *God*. Thus, the task is to display the structure through which all beings are grounded in God. This constitutes for Schelling what can be called, quite literally, pan-theism. The theological aspect is self-evident; since it is this grounding structure that makes human freedom and thus good and evil possible, the ethical aspect also is referred back to the ontological task.

---

4. Schelling begins his *Presentation of My System of Philosophy* (1801) with these words: "After I had attempted for many years to present the one philosophy alone that I know to be true, as philosophy of nature and transcendental philosophy, I now find myself driven by the present situation of science to bring forward publicly sooner than I wished the system itself that for me was the ground of these different presentations." Describing his system as that of the absolute identity of the I (or spirit) and nature, he says in one of his principal propositions: "Everything that is, is absolute identity itself" (*Darstellung meines Systems der Philosophie*, in *Ausgewählte Werke, Schriften von 1801–1804* [Darmstadt: Wissenschaftliche Buchgesellschaft, 1968], 3, 15).

5. Schelling, *Stuttgarter Privatvorlesungen*, in *Ausgewählte Werke, Schriften von 1806–1813*, 380.

The grounding structure can be expressed as an identity in the proposition "God is all." Here the identity asserted by the copula does not mean mere sameness; the two terms of the proposition are not only the same but also different. Even in what might seem a mere assertion of sameness, as in the proposition "A is A," it is a matter of differentiating A from itself in order to cancel the difference and affirm the self-identity of A. In every case, identity designates unification from out of difference. In pantheism (in Schelling's sense), in the proposition "God is all," the difference involved in the identity is that of ground and grounded, and so in this instance the principle of identity converges with the principle of ground (or, in the English designation, the principle of sufficient reason).

Schelling declares that the unity asserted in the proposition "God is all" is "immediately creative."[6] This means that the things grounded in God are not merely mechanical, that "God is not a God of the dead, but of the living."[7] In their procession from God, what they are is not determined; they remain dependent on God, but their dependence does not exclude autonomy. In grounding them, preeminently in grounding humans, God renders them creative rather than determined. But, in turn, this grounding of things does not leave God unaffected: it is precisely through the succession of things that God is revealed to himself. In Schelling's words: "The succession of things from God is a self-revelation of God. But God can reveal himself only in what is like him, in free beings that act by themselves, for whose being there is no ground except God, but who are as God is."[8] These are, then, the two sides of the grounding relation and the unity that binds them in their identity: on the one side, the succession of things from God, from the grounding ground, and on the other side, the self-revelation of God in relation to this succession of things.[9]

Yet, how does God ground this succession? How does this grounding take place? In one respect, Schelling's answer reaches back to the early philosophical appropriation of Christianity, most notably to Augustine. Referring to God and things, Schelling says: "He speaks, and they are there."[10] This expresses the theological-philosophical concep-

---

6. Schelling, *Über das Wesen der menschlichen Freiheit*, 289.
7. Ibid., 290.
8. Ibid., 291.
9. Ibid.
10. Ibid.

tion of creation: that God created the world, not as an artisan might produce something, but rather through the divine λόγος. And yet, as Schelling continues, it turns out that it is not only the divine λόγος that is involved in the grounding of things. Rather, the imagination also plays a role—the divine imagination, which, unlike human imagination, imparts actuality to those things it represents. In introducing imagination in this manner, Schelling is recasting a conception that goes back to Kant and Fichte: that appearances or objects are brought forth through the operation of transcendental imagination. In any case, by ascribing the grounding of things not just to the divine λόγος but also to the divine imagination, Schelling diverges in a very consequential way from the traditional theological-philosophical concept of divine creation.

At the threshold where, observing that everything up to that point has been a "mere introduction," the genuinely systematic part of *On the Essence of Human Freedom* is about to be launched, Schelling invokes the philosophy of nature. He writes that "only from the principles of a true philosophy of nature can a view be developed that is completely sufficient for the task that is to be undertaken."[11] Then, as he is about to introduce the distinction that will govern the entire investigation from this point on, he observes that this distinction has first been established by contemporary philosophy of nature.

Schelling's engagement with the philosophy of nature goes back to the early period when he sought to develop Fichte's *Wissenschaftslehre* in such a way as to account for nature in terms of the Fichtean viewpoint. Both in his *Ideas for a Philosophy of Nature* (1797) and his *Treatise Explaining the Idealism of the Wissenschaftslehre* (1796–97), his intent is to show that objects in nature objectify—that is, display in objective form—the basic activities of spirit. For instance, in the latter text, Schelling draws on Fichte's conception of imagination as involving two basic activities: on the one hand, it is directed outward and extends to infinity; on the other hand, it is directed inward and tends toward a single point. In nature these activities have as their objectifications repulsive and attractive forces, or expansion and concentration. Or again, Schelling writes: "Matter is nothing other than the spirit intuited in the equilibrium of its activities."[12] At this stage Schelling's thought remains within the compass of transcendental philosophy. As such it establishes

---

11. Ibid., 301.
12. Schelling, *Abhandlungen zur Erläuterung des Idealismus der Wissenschaftslehre*, in *Ausgewählte Werke, Schriften von 1794–1798*, 260.

the identity of subject and object, that is, of spirit and nature, not as mere empty sameness but as mediated by the difference between subject and object, between spirit and nature. Nonetheless, as transcendental philosophy it establishes this identity from the side of the subject or of spirit. The identity is, in Hegel's phrase, that of a subjective subject-object.

In the *Introduction to the Outline of a System of the Philosophy of Nature* (1799), there is a decisive development. At this stage transcendental philosophy and philosophy of nature are considered to be coordinate. In Schelling's words: "Now if it is the task of transcendental philosophy to subordinate the real to the ideal, it is, on the other hand, the task of the philosophy of nature to explain the ideal by the real. The two sciences are therefore one science, differentiated only by the opposite orientation of their tasks."[13]

In *On the True Concept of the Philosophy of Nature* (1801), the relation between transcendental philosophy and philosophy of nature is presented as more complex. Most significantly, philosophy of nature is declared to be originary, whereas transcendental philosophy is termed derivative, because "it can never escape the circle of consciousness."[14] This means that within the transcendental purview "the object cannot be seen otherwise than in the moment when it enters consciousness . . ., but never in its primordial origination in the moment when it first comes about."[15] In distinction from transcendental philosophy (or what in this work he calls philosophy of philosophy), Schelling presents philosophy of nature as initiated through an act of abstracting in which one abstracts from that which in the object is subjective, that is, from that which is posited through subjective activity. In this way philosophy of nature (which Schelling now calls pure theoretical philosophy) breaks out of the circle and gains access to the purely objective. In this regard, *purely* objective denotes an objectivity that is neither the mere objectification of subjectivity nor that which, in the opposite direction, is to

---

13. Schelling, *Einleitung zu dem Entwurf eines Systems der Naturphilosophie*, in *Ausgewählte Werke, Schriften von 1799–1801*, 272. This conception of the relation between transcendental philosophy and philosophy of nature is carried over to *System of Transcendental Idealism* (1800). In the Introduction to this work, Schelling writes: "The entire system of philosophy . . . is composed of two basic sciences that, opposed to each other in principle and direction, reciprocally require and complement each other" (*System des transcendentalen Idealismus*, in *Ausgewählte Werke, Schriften von 1799–1801*, 342).

14. Schelling, *Über den wahren Begriff der Naturphilosophie*, in *Ausgewählte Werke, Schriften von 1799–1801*, 641.

15. Ibid., 640f.

be subjectivized so as to render philosophy of nature complementary to transcendental philosophy. Rather, it is a matter of an objectivity that lies outside the circle of subject-object. While the very term *objectivity* thus becomes inappropriate, Schelling can retain the word *nature*, though it can no longer be taken as visible spirit. The name Schelling gives it in *On the Essence of Human Freedom* is *ground*. Ground will be distinguished from existence, and it is around this distinction that the entire development in this text, including its ontological account, will circle.

Thus, by following the development of Schelling's philosophy of nature, it becomes evident why he regards "a true philosophy of nature" as the only view sufficient to the task undertaken in *On the Essence of Human Freedom*. It becomes evident also why he attributes the basic distinction of this work to "contemporary philosophy of nature."

Schelling introduces the distinction first as it applies to God: "Since nothing is prior to or outside God, he must have the ground of his existence within himself."[16] Schelling declares that all philosophies say this but that they speak of this ground only as a mere concept. This is perhaps most evident in the conception of God as *causa sui*. Yet, Schelling insists that ground in God not be treated as a mere concept but as something "real and actual." Thus, he would now put thoroughly in force the demand for ground, the requirement that *every* being be grounded on some grounding-being; this is the requirement expressed in the principle of ground. Hence, even in the case of God, the ground is to be treated *as grounding*, as the basis from which God comes to exist. Instead of merely collapsing the grounding relation in God by reducing it to the virtual identity denoted by *causa sui*, it is necessary to maintain the distinction between God insofar as he exists, that is, God as absolute, and the ground of his existence, which is inseparable (*unabtrennlich*) yet distinguished (*unterschieden*) from God.

Three points need to be noted regarding this fundamental distinction, which governs the entirety of *On the Essence of Human Freedom* from this point on. First of all, it is of the utmost importance to clarify the exact character of the distinction. This is most succinctly expressed in a letter (dated 1812) in which Schelling addresses certain objections raised by Eschenmayer. Here he writes: "But I have not at all spoken of a distinction between *existence* and the ground for existence, but of a distinction between that-which-exists [*dem Existirenden*] and the ground for existence." The letter to Eschenmayer also states quite precisely the

---

16. Schelling, *Über das Wesen der menschlichen Freiheit*, 301.

character of the grounding as it takes place in God: "God has the ground of his existence *in himself*, in his own original essence [*Urwesen*]; thus, this ground belongs to the same original essence to which God as existing (God as the subject of existence) also belongs. In my treatise I identify clearly enough this original essence, from which God himself emerges [*hervortreten*] by the act of his manifestation."[17] Thus, the distinction is not between ground and existence but between ground and that-which-exists, that is, in the present context, God as existing. Both the ground and God as existing belong to the original essence, and it is from the ground belonging to it that God as existing emerges. This emergence takes place in the manifestation of God. As observed already, God becomes manifest to himself in relation to the succession of things.

The second point is that the grounding relation involves a priority: ground is prior to grounded; that is, in the present context, the ground, which is inseparable yet distinguished from God, is prior to God as existing. Schelling specifies that this priority is neither precedence in time nor priority of being. Yet, in the case of God, the priority turns into a kind of circularity, for Schelling writes: "God has within himself an inner ground of his existence, which to this extent precedes him as existing; yet God is just as much prior to the ground insofar as the ground, even as such, could not be if God did not exist *actu*."[18]

The third point concerns nature. Schelling calls the ground of God as existing the *nature* in God. In this conception of nature as in God, he twists to the breaking point the traditional theological-philosophical view that opposes God the creator to nature as the creation. If there is nature in God, then the very concept of God as creator begins to unravel. Schelling proceeds to add a statement about nature that is among the most decisive and consequential in the entire treatise. The statement expresses a determination of precisely what nature is: "nature in general is everything that lies beyond the absolute being of absolute identity."[19] This *beyond* corresponds to that of the *purely objective* to which the development of Schelling's philosophy of nature led. The purely objective breaks out of the circle of subject and object; it lies beyond the circulation

---

17. *Brief an Eschenmayer*, in *Werke: Historisch-kritische Ausgabe*, ed. H. M. Baumgartner, W. G. Jacobs, and H. Krings (Stuttgart: Frommann-Holzboog, 1976ff.), 8:164f. Karl August Eschenmayer was professor of philosophy and medicine at Tübingen. He was at first a disciple of both Jacobi and Schelling but broke with the latter in denying any rational knowledge of the absolute and expounding a mystical philosophy of belief.

18. Schelling, *Über das Wesen der menschlichen Freiheit*, 302.

19. Ibid.

that is charted when transcendental philosophy and philosophy of nature become complementary. Yet, already in that circulation there is broached an *Aufhebung* that would bring subject and object together in a higher unity while also preserving their opposition within this unity. This higher unity is precisely absolute identity, and its mode of being is absolute, is absolute being. Nature is everything that lies beyond absolute identity in its absolute being.

Although Schelling's *Presentation of My System of Philosophy* preceded *On the Essence of Human Freedom* by several years, it has significant bearing on the references to absolute identity in the later work. In one of the principal propositions, Schelling writes: "Absolute identity *is* only under the form of quantitative indifference of the subjective and the objective."[20] Here the identity of subject and object from both the subjective and the objective side is posited at a point of indifference, that is, at a point where there is no directionality whatsoever toward the subjective or the objective. This point of indifference is identified as absolute identity. Since absolute identity unifies the subjective and the objective at the point of indifference, it encompasses everything, both the subjective and the objective, that is, reason and nature. In Schelling's words: "everything that is, is only to the extent that it expresses absolute identity under some determinate form of being."[21] This entails, in turn: "Absolute identity is absolute totality."[22]

If these developments are brought to bear on *On the Essence of Human Freedom*, a basic question is raised. Absolute identity is declared to be the totality of that-which-is. How, then, is it possible for nature to lie beyond absolute identity? How could anything lie beyond absolute identity if it is the totality of that-which-is? This would be possible only for something that has not yet achieved existence, that has not yet quite come to be. Whatever lies beyond absolute identity can only be a kind of proto-being, in distinction from that-which-is. Ground and nature can claim only such proto-being.

Having introduced the fundamental distinction between ground and the existent in relation to God, Schelling then extends the distinction to things, specifically, to the becoming of things. Yet, even this extension still has reference to God: things cannot become in God (in his absoluteness, his existence), since they are infinitely different from him;

---

20. Schelling, *Darstellung meines Systems der Philosophie*, 24.
21. Ibid., 29. See also ibid., 15, and note 4 above.
22. Ibid., 21.

thus, they must become in and from a ground different from God. But since nothing can be outside of God (that is, beyond absolute identity), this ground can only be that within God that is not God himself; that is, it must be from the ground of God's existence that things come to be. The things of nature are born from the nature in God.

What, then, is this ground, this primal nature, this proto-being—granted that it neither *is* nor is a *what*? Schelling describes it by depicting several phenomena in which the workings of the ground come to light.

Ground is longing (*Sehnsucht*), "the longing felt by the eternal one to give birth to itself." Schelling continues: "The longing is not the one itself but is equally eternal with it. It wills to give birth to God, i.e., to unfathomable unity, but to this extent the unity is still not in it itself."[23] This says: the ground is not God as existing, is not absolute identity, is distinguished from though inseparable from God, who as existing is the one itself. As longing, the ground wills—or is the will—to give birth to God as existing, though the unity that belongs to God is not possessed by the ground. Though the longing is will, it is not yet a will that contains understanding (*Verstand*), not the will of God as existing, but rather an intimating will (*ein ahndender Wille*). Yet, in whatever form, the ground is the nature in God. It is nature, then, that would—that wills, that longs to—give birth to existent God. Such birth would be a birth from nature, a birth of nature (subjective genitive). Grounding thus takes the form of giving birth. With this determination of grounding as giving birth, Schelling breaks with its determination as production (ποίησις), which has remained dominant throughout most of the history of philosophy.

Schelling also describes the ground *as it remains* after the birth of God and the becoming of things. He writes: "After the eternal act of self-revelation, all is rule, order, and form in the world as we now see it. But the unruly [*das Regellose*] always still lies in the ground, as if it could break through once again, and nowhere does it appear as though order and form were originary but rather as if something initially unruly had been brought to order. This is the incomprehensible basis of reality in things, the emergent remainder, that which with the greatest exertion cannot be resolved into understanding but remains eternally in the ground."[24] The consequences of what is said in this remarkable passage are unlimited—just as the passage itself announces the unlimited, the unruly. As a whole, the passage concerns the double priority of the

---

23. Schelling, *Über das Wesen der menschlichen Freiheit*, 303.
24. Ibid., 303f.

ground, that is, of unruly nature. First of all, it is declared that the unruly ground rather than rule and order is originary (*das Ursprüngliche*, which translates ἀρχή). It is *from* the unruly ground that rule and order first come about. But also, secondly, even after rule and order have come to be, the unruly is not simply eliminated but remains; it persists as a remainder. As such it is irreducible to divine understanding, to absolute identity, and so is beyond absolute identity. It remains as if it could break through once again; it is like something repressed that eventually breaks through all that—like the forces of order—would repress it and that in its return, in this return of nature, returns still more powerfully. No doubt Schelling knew of the return of eros in deed that is announced at the end of the *Symposium* by the arrival of Alcibiades.

Schelling describes the ground also as darkness. Grounding is, then, birth from the darkness of longing into the light of understanding. He says even that "all birth is birth from darkness into light."[25] He writes also that this originary, dark longing "moves forebodingly like an undulating, surging sea, similar to Plato's matter."[26] The reference is to the receptacle (ὑποδοχή) or, among its various names, χώρα. It is also called mother, and it is likely that this designation was for Schelling the most significant, as denoting the birth-giving capacity of the ground.

As the counterpart or progeny of the ground (longing, unruly, nature, darkness), there is engendered in God a reflective representation, a representation of God to himself, a representation through which "God beholds himself in his own image."[27] With this representation, God as absolute is born, and thus there comes to fulfillment what in the ground was mere intimating longing. This representation constitutes understanding (*Verstand*) and generates the word. Consequently, what was merely longed for but remained in darkness comes to be thought (to think itself) in understanding and to be expressed, to be named, in the word. There emerges spirit and love, the most originary forces of unification. Ground and representation, longing and understanding, nature and spirit are joined as the word is uttered and form is given to the

---

25. Ibid., 304.
26. Ibid. See *Timaeus* 47e–71d. As early as 1792, two years before his first published work, Schelling occupied himself with the *Timaeus* and during this period produced a notebook recording his studies. This notebook has been published along with related material in Schelling, *Timaeus (1794)*, ed. Hartmut Buchner (Stuttgart-Bad Cannstadt: Frommann-Holzboog, 1994). See my discussion in *Chorology: On Beginning in Plato's "Timaeus"* (Bloomington: Indiana University Press, 1999), 155–67.
27. Schelling, *Über das Wesen der menschlichen Freiheit*, 304f.

originarily unruly nature. And yet, beneath the form that representation, understanding, spirit, and the word bequeath to unruly nature, it persists, it is not assimilated, and it threatens to break through the order and form that have been established.

The birth of God as his self-revelation belongs together with the creation of things, with the release of their succession. Both proceed from the unruly ground, from the nature in God. In the ground this dual birth, of God and of the things of nature, is already anticipated. Schelling writes: "Now because this being (initial nature [*die anfängliche Natur*]) is nothing other than the eternal ground of God's existence, it must contain within itself, although sealed up [*verschlossen*], the essence of God as a gleaming spark of life in the darkness of the deep."[28]

In the account of the birth of the things of nature along with the designation of the ground as the initial nature (*die anfängliche Natur*) and later in this text as the old nature (*die alte Natur*), Schelling reopens a distinction that was decisive for the Greek thinkers up through Aristotle but that was largely effaced in the subsequent history of philosophy. The distinction is that between nature as such (φύσις) and natural things (τὰ φύσει ὄντα). The relation between these, the grounding of natural things on nature as such, is a matter of giving birth. It is the birth of nature, in both senses of the genitive.

Within the ground, says Schelling, the essence of God lies sealed up as a spark of life in the darkness. While the ground strives to keep this spark of life sealed up, divine self-understanding sets out to raise this concealed essence from the depths, to let this spark fly up into the open. And yet—though Schelling leaves it unsaid at this point—the ground as nature, as mother, continues to draw the progeny to itself; that is, conversely, it threatens to break through into the open and in its concealment to contain the flame that has flared up.

Finally, Schelling describes—or rather, names—the connection between the two births of nature. It is forged by a process that he names *true imagination* (*wahre Ein-bildung*), "whereby what arises is imaged into nature [*in die Natur hineingebildet wird*]."[29] This says: what is raised out of the depth is imaged into nature (into the succession of natural things as they come to be ordered). On the one side, this imaging into is the creation—or what takes the place of creation—of natural things;

---

28. Ibid., 305.
29. Ibid., 305f.

on the other side, it is in this natural image that God beholds himself so that his self-revelation comes to pass.

The ontology that Schelling develops in *On the Essence of Human Freedom* has the effect of twisting the classical grounding structure to the point where it is finally thrown out of joint. According to the classical structure, things are referred back to God as their ground, and their grounding takes the form of production, even if simply by means of the word. Yet this order of grounding merely extends what was already expounded by the Greeks: that sensible, natural things are grounded in their intelligible paradigms. Even God himself, in thinking the intelligible, is grounded, namely, in himself and so is characterized as *causa sui*. Schelling's decisive move is to distinguish between God as existing and the ground of God as existing. Thus, both God as existing and the becoming of things are referred back to this ground (old nature, initial nature, the nature in God) that is distinct from God. Ground is conceived, then, as utterly different from the classical conception of ground—as becomes evident in Schelling's descriptions of it as longing, as the unruly, as the darkness of the depth. Therefore, God can no longer be designated as the creator, who would fashion the world according to the paradigm of production. Furthermore, grounding can no longer be conceived as the inverse of creation, as the grounding of the sensible on the intelligible. Rather, grounding now has the character of giving birth; it is the birth of nature. God can no longer be regarded as *causa sui* but rather as progeny of the ground, as given birth by nature. In the final analysis, natural things also are given birth by nature itself, as what emerges from the ground is imaged into nature, so that it is through imagination (rethought ontologically), not by thought and the word, that natural things emerge in their succession. It is only in coordination with this succession that God achieves self-revelation, that is, comes to exist.

The consequences of these fundamental reconfigurations are virtually unlimited. Since God is now conceived neither as creator of nature nor as origin of himself, as *causa sui*, he is set back upon the sealed-off ground, which is distinguished from him. Since this ground is what gives birth to God, it is anterior to him; it is more originary. To this extent the ontological status of God is no different from that of natural things, since both are given birth by the ground. The superiority of God, his ruling over nature, over natural things, is cancelled once and for all. But this ontological reduction of God consists not only in his being set

THE BIRTH OF NATURE   43

back upon the ground as that which gives birth to him; he is also contaminated by the ground. Since the ground, though distinguished from God, is also in God, its darkness cannot but overtake and diminish the light, indeed the very source of light, undermining thereby the intelligibility that has since antiquity characterized God and rendered him the ground of sensible, natural things.

As the withdrawn, concealed ἀρχή of all beings, the ground draws along with it into the dark depth the being that was once called God but for whom perhaps another name has now to be invented, perhaps even a name evocative of certain traits of the Greek mythical figures.

It would, then, be necessary to reconceive this being—perhaps even as no longer conceivable as a being—in his peculiar affinity and interlacement with the ground. There would remain only this configuration, for which the seclusion of the ground would be decisive, and, secured within and upon this configuration, the event of manifestation in which imagination (reconfigured ontologically) would let the things of nature come forth.

3 RETURN TO NATURE

What is to be heard in the phrase "Return to nature"?

Taken most directly, the phrase expresses an imperative. Suppose that it is addressed to someone, or even that in solitude one addresses it to oneself. On those to whom it is addressed it imposes the demand that they return to nature. As the condition of its pertinence, the imperative presupposes that its addressees either have themselves retreated from nature or have somehow been withdrawn from it, so that in either case they are separated or at least distanced from nature. The imperative enjoins them to return across this distance, to close the space of separation, so as to come again into proximity to nature, so as to arrive once more at the place where they would once have been, even if in a past that would never quite have been present.

And yet, in completing such an odyssey, they would come to occupy this place differently. Once immediacy has been disrupted, even if always already, the situation is never again the same as it would have been. Once, having been set apart, they return to nature, they will have reinstalled themselves therein with a certain deliberateness; they will perdure within the compass of nature only through resolve, and thus always with a certain residual detachment. The trajectory through which they will have passed will always have left its trace in their comportment.

The imperative to return to nature has been repeatedly sounded in the history of philosophy, and the heterogeneity of its sources is indicative of the manifold senses borne by the phrase. It is voiced already in antiquity. It receives one of its most direct expressions in the contrast that Diogenes of Sinope drew between convention and nature and in his insistence that happiness depends on acting in accordance with nature.¹ The human in search of happiness is thus enjoined to measure his actions by reference to nature, by turning—or returning—to nature as his guide. According to ancient testimony, both Chrysippus and Diogenes of Babylon declared that choice, as in selecting some things and rejecting others, should be exercised in accordance with nature, that is, again, by turning—or returning—to nature as guide.² Reporting the precepts of the Stoics, Stobaeus writes: "All things in accordance with nature are to-be-taken, and all things contrary to nature are not-to-be-taken." And again: "All things in accordance with nature have worth, and all things contrary to nature are unworthy."³ The theme is pervasive from the early Cynics throughout much of Stoicism: the measure of actions, of things, and of their worth is to be found by turning—or returning—to nature, by determining whether they are in accordance with nature (κατὰ φύσιν).

Thus, the return to nature may be carried out in order to secure a proper measure; actions and dealings with things will then be executed in accord with nature, will be fitted to its measure. Yet the very concept of measure, the differentiation between what provides the measure and what is measured by it, indicates that these instances of human comportment retain a residual detachment from nature itself. They are to be measured by nature, not assimilated to it.

The return to nature, as demanded in the imperative, may be carried out in other ways, that is, with other ends in view and in various registers. In the mid-eighteenth century the imperative was sounded in a form unheard-of in antiquity. In his *Discourse on the Origin and Basis of Inequality among Men*—the so-called *Second Discourse*—Rousseau undertook to return descriptively to the human as it existed in its original—that is, savage—stage, in what Rousseau calls the state of nature (*l'état de nature*). In recovering and describing the human in the state of nature, his intent is to show how, once humans left this state and the development of society commenced, human inequality and hence

---

1. See Émile Bréhier, *The Hellenistic and Roman Age*, trans. Wade Baskin (Chicago: University of Chicago Press, 1965), 13–16.
2. *The Hellenistic Philosophers*, ed. with translations and commentary by A. A. Long and D. N. Sedley (Cambridge: Cambridge University Press, 1987), 1:356–57.
3. Ibid., 1:355 (translation modified). Greek text is given in ibid., 2:350–51.

oppression and injustice came about. Here, then, the return to nature is theoretical; it is a matter not of modern men again becoming savages, but only of describing that original state. The description of the state of nature is meant, in turn, to serve a political end, or at least to enable an analysis of modern social-political conditions, of the means by which the inequality in modern society came about. Yet, in turn, this analysis identifies the customs, laws, and institutions that would need to be dissolved or at least radically transformed in order to eliminate inequality and establish a society in which, as was the case with humans in the state of nature, all are equal. Thus, Rousseau's descriptive return to nature opens the way to a condition that, though not that of the savage, would, in a way accordant with modern life, approximate the state of nature.

Yet within the scope of this return to nature, Rousseau also carries out other, more specific modes of return, returning to nature in other registers. One such register is that of the origin of language. In Rousseau's description of the human condition in the state of nature, it becomes evident that as long as humans were living in such proximity to nature, they had little or no need for language; they had "no laws other than those of nature, no language other than that of gesture and some inarticulate sounds."[4] Only at the threshold of the break with the state of nature did incipient speech first appear, namely, as what Rousseau calls "the cry of nature [*le cri de la nature*]," which was uttered only in situations of great danger or violent pain.[5] Later, other sounds besides the mere cry were added: the inflections of the voice were multiplied and combined with gestures. Still later, in order to overcome the limitation of gestures, our progenitors introduced articulate vocal sounds, and language in the proper sense thus began to develop. Hence, through his descriptive return to nature, to humans in the state of nature, Rousseau provides the basis for his account of the origin and development of language.

---

4. Jean-Jacques Rousseau, *Essay on the Origin of Languages*, in *Essay on the Origin of Languages and Writings Related to Music* (Hanover, NH: University Press of New England, 1998), 305. The final version of this text dates from 1762, though it was not published until after Rousseau's death. It was originally a fragment from the *Second Discourse*, which Rousseau omitted as too long and out of place.

5. Rousseau, *Discourse on the Origin and Basis of Inequality among Men*, in *The Essential Rousseau* (New York: New American Library, 1974), 159. Originally published in 1755.

Another register in which Rousseau carries out the return to nature is that of music. The proposal for such a return is set against the background of the intense debate in mid-eighteenth-century France over the relative merits of French and Italian music. The so-called "Quarrel of the Bouffons" was occasioned when an Italian troupe came to Paris and performed Pergolesi's *La Serva Padrona* with great success. Rousseau's response was his *Letter on French Music*, which was extremely critical of French music and its reliance on complex harmonies, as in the music of Rameau, in contrast to the simpler melodies of Italian music. Rousseau becomes a staunch advocate of melody and of the unity of melody. He writes: "It is therefore a certain principle and one founded in nature that every music in which the harmony is scrupulously filled out, every accompaniment in which all the chords are complete, must produce a great deal of noise, but have very little expressiveness."[6] By contrast: the Italians demonstrate "that the great art of the composer consists no less in knowing how to discern at the time the notes he should omit than those he should use."[7]

In his *Essay on the Origin of Languages*, which in its full title bears the further designation "In Which Melody and Musical Imitation Are Treated," Rousseau focuses on another phase in the development of language. It is a phase that he presents by depicting a kind of primal scene at a fountain or a festival where the passions of lovers-to-be are aroused and speech first flourishes, first comes fully into its own. Here is his imaginary depiction of how language originated around the fountains: "There were formed the first ties between families; there the first meetings between the two sexes took place. Young girls came to fetch water for the household; young men came to water their herds. Their eyes, accustomed to the same objects from childhood, began to see sweeter ones. The heart was moved by these new objects, an unfamiliar attraction made it less savage; it felt the pleasure of not being alone. Imperceptibly water became more necessary; the livestock were thirsty more often; they arrived in haste and parted reluctantly. . . . There the first festivals took place, feet leaped with joy, eager gesture no longer sufficed, the voice accompanied it with passionate accents."[8]

---

6. Rousseau, *Letter on French Music*, in *Essay on the Origin of Languages and Writings Related to Music*, 161. Originally published in 1753.

7. Ibid., 162.

8. Rousseau, *Essay on the Origin of Languages*, in *Essay on the Origin of Languages and Writings Related to Music*, 314.

48 THE RETURN OF NATURE

According to Rousseau, it was here, along the way from the state of nature, that music was born. As it arose, it consisted solely of melody and was bound closely to speech. This was, as it were, music's state of nature.⁹ What came later was, perhaps even more than in society at large, a matter of degeneration: with the rationalization of language, separation ensued between speech and song; then, as harmony became dominant, melody—and hence song—was impaired, so that finally there resulted an expressionless music forgetful of the voice. Need it be said that through this analysis Rousseau is proposing a return by which music would come into proximity to its state of nature? Then melody would again become primary, harmony serving only for its enhancement; and song, thus restored, would again follow the accents of speech.

This is a proposal that Rousseau not only declared but also, as composer, sought to carry out, as in his celebrated opera *The Wizard of the Village* (*Le Devin du Village*).¹⁰ The theme of the opera is the triumph of spontaneous simplicity and virtue over the corruption of the noble classes. The story is a simple tale about a shepherd and a shepherdess. Abandoned by her lover, Colin, who has set out to seduce the mistress of the noble estate, Colette seeks the aid of the wizard, whose simple scheme reunites the lovers. The opera ends with dancing and joy. It is, then, a plot that celebrates the return to a simpler, more natural form of life, a return of life to nature. Especially striking is the manner in which the music exemplifies Rousseau's views regarding music. It is composed in such a style as to express the feelings of the characters, the sentiments and passions evoked by their situation. The emphasis is on melody. The choral singing is often in unison rather than harmony. All the harmonies and embellishments that are included are intended to enhance rather than stifle the melody.

In some instances a return to nature is broached within a highly determined register and within a larger context committed contrariwise

---

9. It is only by analogy that one can ascribe a state of nature to music. For Rousseau regards music as intrinsically distanced from nature. Thus, contrasting it with painting, he writes: "One sees from this that painting is closer to nature and that music depends more on human art" (*Essay on the Origin of Languages*, in *Essay on the Origin of Languages and Writings Related to Music*, 326).

10. *The Wizard of the Village* was performed at Fontainebleau in 1752 before the king, and then in 1753 at the Paris Opera. It proved to be one of the most popular operas of the eighteenth century. By the end of the century, there had been around four hundred performances. Rousseau later attributed its success to the perfect accord between the words and the music and especially to its "hidden principle," the unity of melody.

to separation from nature. Consider the case of Kant. Although the *Critique of Pure Reason* begins by acknowledging the dependence of knowledge on experience, the primary movement enacted in the critical project consists in a regress from experience—primarily from the experience of nature—to the *a priori* conditions of such experience, conditions that lie not in nature but in the subject. This directionality expresses the very sense of Kant's so-called Copernican Revolution. The movement counter to nature is even more pronounced in Kant's practical philosophy: morality itself lies in self-determination that, utterly detached from natural inclination, is carried out in accordance with the moral law.

It is only in the *Critique of Judgment* that an exception is found, one that is all the more striking in that it occurs within a context in which, even as the beauty of natural things is discussed, there remain moments of retreat from nature. The relevant passage is that in which Kant affirms the contemplation of nature, or, more precisely, intellectual interest in the beautiful in nature. Such interest attests, according to Kant, to a mental attunement to moral feeling; for a person so attuned will always take an interest in any trace that nature provides of its harmony with our own spirit and its law. It is precisely such a trace that nature offers in the purposiveness of its beauty. On this basis Kant declares natural beauty superior to the beauty of art. The return to nature, as the turn from art to nature, he then expresses in a single, very remarkable sentence depicting the scene of such a return: "A man who has taste enough to judge the products of fine art with the greatest correctness and refinement may still be glad to leave a room in which he finds those beauties that minister to vanity and perhaps to social joys, and to turn instead to the beautiful in nature, in order to find there, as it were, a voluptuousness for his spirit in a train of thought that he can never fully lay out."[11]

That the trace of spirit is to be found in nature, through the return to nature, is a theme that resonates throughout post-Kantian thought, and in particular with the New England transcendentalists. Emerson echoes the Kantian theme of the purposiveness displayed by the beauty of nature but extends it by declaring that any reflection into oneself requires also an outward turn, which may indeed be oriented to the beauty of nature but which may instead be directed to a portion of nature that is remote and inaccessible, as when, looking at the stars, one is

---

11. Immanuel Kant, *Kritik der Urteilskraft*, in vol. 5 of *Werke: Akademie Textausgabe*, 299f.

enabled to turn back into solitude. Furthermore, Emerson's concept of nature—at least what he calls the common concept—is broadened to the point where it includes not only things and the processes in which they undergo exchange with one another, but also the elements—air, ocean, earth, the sky in its brilliance, the fourfold course of the year. Emerson says that in all these forms we take delight.

To be sure, there is also a tendency in Emerson's thought toward what he calls the philosophical sense of nature, according to which natural things and elements would serve primarily for the self-manifestation of spirit. Yet, while emphasizing the dependence of nature on spirit, to this extent degrading nature, he insists that spirit also depends on nature for its self-manifestation. There is, then, a certain crossing of the two senses of nature and an ambivalence as regards the relation of dependence between spirit and nature.

And yet, Emerson repeatedly declares, we take delight in nature; and so, at least on one side of the ambivalence, the return of nature to spirit opens also the space of a return from spirit to nature, to the surplus, the remainder, by which nature would exceed spirit. It is by entering into this surplus of nature that the human spirit can be expanded and enhanced by nature rather than simply reducing it to a material to serve human ends.

It is appropriate to cite some lines from the poem that Emerson places at the head of his essay "Nature":

> The rounded world is fair to see,
> Nine times folded in mystery
> . . . .
> Spirit that lurks each form within
> Beckons to spirit of its kin.[12]

For Emerson the human spirit is expanded by coming into proximity to nature, by returning from the detachment from nature inculcated and enforced by city life. In the essay "Nature," he describes the return from the city to nature: "At the gates of the forest, the surprised man of the world is forced to leave his city estimates of great and small, wise and foolish. The knapsack of custom falls off his back with the first step he takes into these precincts. Here is sanctity which shames our religions, and reality which discredits our heroes. Here we find Nature to be the

---

12. Ralph Waldo Emerson, "Nature," in *Selected Writings*, 406. This essay belongs to the Second Series, which was originally published in 1844.

circumstance which dwarfs every other circumstance, and judges like a god all men that come to her."[13]

Thoreau also writes of nature in such a way, though in a more exclamatory style, as near the beginning of *Walden*: "To anticipate, not the sunrise and the dawn merely, but, if possible, Nature herself!"[14] Other passages attest to his euphoria in the presence of nature: "The indescribable innocence and beneficence of Nature,—of sun and wind and rain, of summer and winter,—such health, such cheer, they afford forever!"[15] Thoreau stresses that city life, even village life, has need of a certain proximity to the wildness of nature: "Our village life would stagnate if it were not for the unexplored forests and meadows which surround it. We need the tonic of wildness."[16] *Walden* also abounds with laconic expressions of Thoreau's experience of nature: "A lake is the landscape's most beautiful and expressive feature. It is earth's eye; looking into which the beholder measures the depth of his own nature."[17] Yet what is most distinctive in the case of Thoreau is that he enacted the return to nature, living alone for two years in the woods on the shore of Walden Pond and transcribing that enactment in his book *Walden*.

In all these instances the pertinence of the imperative to return to nature is based to a certain extent on the capacity of nature to set before human sensibility a trace of spirit. From nature one is displayed to oneself in some specific manner: as submitted to measure, as spirit, or in the originary form that characterized the human in the state of nature. Yet, it is not only for the sake of self-discovery that the return to nature is carried out. It is equally for the sake of encountering the wildness of nature, which, in our very experience of belonging to it, shows that it is once and for all set apart from us—like the remote, inaccessible stars. In the return to nature, we encounter the wildness that abounds in nature—as in the eyes of a wild animal. The return to nature also awakens a sense of the elemental in nature and of our incapacity to master and control it, to turn it into a means by which to achieve merely human aims. While the ocean, the air, and the earth can indeed be exploited or contaminated, they continue to exceed immeasurably the human

---

13. Ibid. Regarding Emerson's concept of nature and of the ambivalent relation between nature and spirit, see the discussion above in chap. 1.

14. Henry David Thoreau, *Walden*, ed. Brooks Atkinson (New York: Random House, 1965), 15. Originally published in 1854.

15. Ibid., 125.

16. Ibid., 283.

17. Ibid., 168.

sphere. In all these forms and many others, nature withdraws as at the same time it draws us along as belonging to nature.

In German Idealism the conception of nature as serving for the self-disclosure of spirit is paramount. Nature thus comes to be thought as the idea in its otherness, in an externality—indeed as externality itself—to be cancelled as spirit emerges in its self-disclosure. The return to nature occurs only for the sake of the return, in turn, from nature back to spirit; in this ultimate return nature is cancelled as mere nature, is relieved of its nature, and is brought back to spirit, raised to the level of spirit.

And yet, this is not the only motif in German Idealism. As shown above (chap. 1), there are in Hegel certain fissures through which nature installs itself in spirit while remaining nature, that is, without being assimilated to spirit. This other motif comes to be developed and indeed becomes dominant in Schelling's 1809 work on human freedom. Specifically, when nature is determined as what lies beyond the absolute being of absolute identity, that is, beyond the sphere in which it would be superseded by spirit, Schelling posits nature as withdrawn from spirit, as irreducibly beyond any assimilation by spirit (see chap. 2).

The determination of nature as both other than spirit and yet none other than spirit is reflected in the double sense borne by the word. For one speaks not only of nature but also of the nature of things, even of the nature of nature. On the one side, the word designates the domain of natural things—mountains and rivers, trees and flowers—which is regarded as quite apart from the spiritual, but on the other side, it designates what something essentially is, its essence, which in modern thought is intrinsically allied with subjectivity or spirit. Yet, this double sense of nature extends back to Greek antiquity: already in the Platonic dialogues the word φύσις is commonly used in both senses. In its broader application, the word signifies, on the one side, the domain or origin of natural things and, on the other side, the εἴδη that define all such things, that determine them to be what they are, thus constituting the answer to the question: τί ἐστι? As correlative to νόησις, the εἴδη are designated as νοητά, as what comes to be called the intelligible; and the intelligible is then distinguished from the αἰσθητά, the sensible. The dyad of intelligible and sensible that is thus designated comes, therefore, to encompass in its span the entire range of being, and as such it provides the founding distinction of what comes to be called metaphysics. In its double sense nature enjoys the same gigantic span. Nothing lies

RETURN TO NATURE 53

outside this span, neither beyond it nor before it. Nothing lies outside of nature. Hence, the return to nature will always be also a return within nature.

And yet, both in classical antiquity and in our time, this ontological configuration has been disrupted. This disruption of the intelligible/sensible dyad involves, though in very different ways, the emergence of another sense of nature.

In classical antiquity this disruption occurs, in its most manifest form, in Plato's *Timaeus*. In the account given of how the godly δημιουργός formed the cosmos, the dyad of intelligible and sensible is affirmed and indeed is woven into the entire first discourse that Timaeus delivers. And yet, precisely at the point where the discourse focuses most intently on the order in the heaven, a certain disordering begins to announce itself. As a result, Timaeus interrupts his discourse and proposes to begin again from the beginning. In the second discourse, which then follows, this interruption proves to have been the interruption of the intelligible/sensible dyad. Not that Timaeus rejects the dyad or in any way puts it aside; rather, along with these two kinds, the intelligible and the sensible, he introduces a third kind. Thereby he demonstrates both that the dyad is not comprehensive, that it does not encompass the entire range of being, and that its very possibility is based on the third kind.

The third kind is named in numerous ways, all of which—even the designation "third kind"—are necessarily consigned to what Timaeus terms bastard discourse. Timaeus declares it to be like gold that can be molded into all possible shapes. He also calls it by the name ἐκμαγεῖον, which designates a mass of wax or other soft material on which the imprint of a seal can be stamped. He calls it also ὑποδοχή, commonly translated as "receptacle," and, most insistently, by the name χώρα. These different designations are cast in such a way that they clash and utterly resist being brought together into a single image of a certain kind. For what is being named—in a necessarily bastardly way—is neither a kind, that is, an intelligible εἶδος, nor an image of a kind, that is, a sensible thing.

The word φύσις is scattered throughout the *Timaeus* and is used in several different senses. Early in the dialogue Timaeus is described as one who has made it his task to know "about the nature of the all [περὶ φύσεως τοῦ παντός]."[18] Much later, when Timaeus actually enumerates

---

18. Plato, *Timaeus* 27a.

the three kinds, he refers to the offspring, that is, the sensible, as the φύσις between the other two.[19] But among the many usages of the word, there are two that are especially significant in the present context. One is exemplified when Timaeus speaks "about the nature that receives all bodies [περὶ τῆς τὰ πάντα δεχομένης σώματα φύσεως]."[20] In this phrase it is the third kind that is designated as nature, as a nature other than the nature that Timaeus described in his first discourse. The other usage occurs when, as he proposes to begin again, Timaeus enjoins his interlocutors that "We must bring into view the nature itself [φύσιν . . . αὐτήν] of fire and water, and air and earth, before the birth of the heaven."[21] The reference is to what will prove to be not the elements themselves, but rather the elements as not yet themselves, as mere traces (ἴχνοι) held in the χώρα. This entire scene lies before the birth of the heaven; it is a nature that preceded nature, a nature older than sensible nature.

The classical ontological configuration is also disrupted in our time, that is, from Nietzsche on. This disruption is encapsulated in a single sentence in the Prologue to *Thus Spoke Zarathustra*. It is a performative utterance that borders on issuing an imperative. It reads: "I beseech you, my brothers, *remain true to the earth* [bleibt der Erde treu], and do not believe those who speak to you of otherworldly hopes!"[22] Here the earth represents the things of the earth, that is, the sensible; and the otherworld represents the intelligible, now that, in Nietzsche's idiom, this allegedly true world, the otherworldly, has finally become a fable. What the sentence announces is thus an inversion of the classical configuration, an inversion by which the sensible is now to be regarded as the true world, while the intelligible is allowed to drift away into oblivion, that is, is abolished. There remains—so it seems—only the sensible, only nature in the sense of the sensible. It is to this nature, the only nature, that Nietzsche implores his brothers to return. To philosophize after Nietzsche would require a return to the nature in which there are mountains and rivers, trees and flowers.

And yet, in Nietzsche's celebrated account of how the true world finally became a fable, the abolition of the intelligible constitutes only the

---

19. Ibid. 50d.
20. Ibid. 50b.
21. Ibid. 48b.
22. Friedrich Nietzsche, *Also Sprach Zarathustra*, in vol. VI/1 of *Werke: Kritische Gesamtausgabe* (Berlin: Walter de Gruyter, 1968), 9.

penultimate stage. What follows in the final stage thoroughly disrupts the direct and seemingly self-evident return to nature that would seem to be prescribed. Here is Nietzsche's account of the final stage: "The true world we have abolished. What world has remained? The apparent one perhaps? But no! *With the true world we have also abolished the apparent one.*"[23] Yet, what is the sense of this final graphic deed, this claim to have abolished the apparent—that is, the sensible—world? For most, certainly, the sensible world is not, in its actuality, abolished; it is not done away with. We open our eyes or attune our ears, and—behold!—the things of sense are there before us. While it may be that the intelligible, since it was never more than a specter, has vanished completely and has only to be put out of our minds, erased from our memory, the sensible stubbornly persists in its perceptibility and in its support of and resistance to our endeavors.

What is it, then, about the sensible that has been abolished? It is only—and precisely—its character as apparent, as *scheinbar*, as appearance (*Erscheinung*) of something beyond it, namely, of the intelligible. Because since classical antiquity the sensible has always been understood by reference to the intelligible, the abolition of the intelligible deprives the sensible of the determination it has borne throughout the history of metaphysics. Now that it can no longer be understood as imaging the intelligible, the sensible is utterly lacking in determination. Now that it stands alone, there is no telling what it is, not at least in a discourse that continues to be governed by the conceptuality of metaphysics. Now that there remains only the nature in which there are mountains and rivers, trees and flowers, the very sense of nature must be determined anew. Now we must—like Timaeus—begin again from the beginning.

A beginning can be discerned in certain directions taken in the development of phenomenology from Heidegger on. Responding to the Nietzschean injunction, *Being and Time* sets sensible beings free of the intelligible. No longer are they determined as imaging a remote intelligible set beyond them, nor as grounded in the pure concepts of a transcendental subject or of spirit. Rather, they are taken as determined by their insertion in a world, by their placement within the referential structures that constitute a world. The world itself is nothing set beyond the sensible beings within it. Without itself being a sensible being, it belongs nonetheless to the domain of the sensible; it is *of* the sensible even

---

23. Nietzsche, *Götzen-Dämmerung*, in vol. VI/3 of *Werke: Kritische Gesamtausgabe* (Berlin: Walter de Gruyter, 1969), 75.

though not itself a sensible being. Though in Heidegger's early thought the world is intrinsically bound to the human, this bond is not a grounding, nor is the human taken as a transcendental subject or as spirit. In the development of Heidegger's thought that begins in *Contributions to Philosophy*, even this bond is broken, and whatever affinity there might have been with the metaphysics of the subject is eliminated. Merleau-Ponty's conception of the invisible, as that which, without itself being visible, belongs to and indeed renders possible the visible, extends and develops the redetermination of the sensible that frees it from governance by an intelligible beyond.

But what does this beginning ventured in phenomenology entail with regard to the determination of the sense of nature? Is nature to be regarded simply as the totality of sensible beings? Most certainly it was not so regarded by the ancients. Even in Aristotle the distinction persists between nature and natural things, between φύσις and τὰ φύσει ὄντα; nature itself Aristotle defines as an inner ἀρχή that governs the origination and growth of natural things. While the *Timaeus* does sometimes employ the word φύσις in reference to sensible beings, it also applies the word to other kinds such as the χώρα that are rigorously distinguished from sensible beings. Kant, too, avoids simply identifying nature with the totality of sensible beings. In a highly significant footnote in the *Critique of Pure Reason*, he distinguishes between a formal or adjectival sense of nature and a material or substantive sense. Nature in the latter sense he identifies as "the sum of appearances insofar as . . . they are thoroughly interconnected." These are, says Kant, "the things of nature," while nature itself is "a subsisting whole [*ein bestehendes Ganzes*]." He distinguishes this sense of nature from the formal sense, according to which nature designates "the connection of the determinations of a thing according to an inner principle of causality." Hence, nature in the formal sense is not a totality of beings but rather the connection (*Zusammenhang*) between their determinations. Nature in this sense consists not of beings, but of the connection by which they are determined as what they are. It is because of its bearing on *what* things are that Kant links nature in this sense to such expressions as "the nature of fluid matter, of fire, etc."[24]

In view of these historical indications, the question needs to be addressed as to whether there are discernible moments or entities that, while intrinsically related to sensible beings, nonetheless are distinct

---

24. Kant, *Kritik der reinen Vernunft*, in vol. 3 of *Werke*, A419 / B446.

from them. Is it possible, beyond the structure of world and the conception of the invisible, to discern and determine moments, configurations, or even entities that go beyond—that exceed—the domain of sensible beings, that lie outside it, such that, if nature is to include these, it cannot be identified simply as the totality of sensible beings?

There are at least two such moments or kinds of entities that can be discerned. Each has the effect of rendering nature as something in excess of the mere totality of sensible beings. One has come to light very recently; the other is to be retrieved from very ancient sources.

The first corresponds to the discovery in recent astrophysics of beings that are not sensible, that by their very nature cannot be presented to sense. Among the several instances of such beings, the most obtrusively excessive are black holes. Such beings have a structure that in no way corresponds to that of a terrestrial thing, of a being having sensibly perceptible properties. Because of its enormous density, the gravity of a black hole is so powerful that even light cannot escape the event horizon that defines its extent. Since no light can escape it, the black hole is completely invisible and can be detected only indirectly, for example, by the shower of particles that is produced in its vicinity.[25] Its invisibility is of a kind never before known; indeed it is an invisibility that is virtually inconceivable by means of the ontological categories operative in Western philosophy since the Greeks. Most significantly, it cannot in any way be present to sense. Its being—if even this category can still be employed—is not that of a sensible being. Yet, situated as it is, as all black holes are, among sensible beings, for example, at the center of at least some galaxies, a black hole presumably belongs to nature. This belonging expands the concept of nature beyond that of the totality of sensible beings.

The second of the moments or entities by which nature exceeds the mere totality of sensible beings can be discerned by taking up the connection drawn in the *Timaeus* between nature, especially in the sense of the χώρα, and the traces of the elements. This connection points back to the elemental thinking of early Greek philosophers such as Anaximenes, Heraclitus, and especially Empedocles; for all these figures, thinking is, as such, directed to φύσις, and φύσις is thought primarily as the gathering of the elements.[26] Engagement with these ancient sources prompts

25. See the more extensive discussion below in chap. 6. See also my discussion in *Logic of Imagination: The Expanse of the Elemental* (Bloomington: Indiana University Press, 2012), chap. 7.

26. See my discussion in *The Figure of Nature* (Bloomington: Indiana University Press, 2016), chaps. 2–4.

a renewal of the sense of element, of element in the sense still heard when we speak of being exposed to the elements. Even the elements named by the ancients, in names barely translatable as fire, air, water, and earth, open toward senses that resist appropriation by metaphysics: elements such as light and sky, wind and rain, the sea, the earth. These expand the sense of nature, not—as with black holes—by being non-sensible, not by remaining withdrawn from sense. On the contrary, though differentiated from sensible things,[27] the elements surround us and are eminently displayed before our senses—in the blue of the sky, the brilliance of the light, the coolness of the wind, the sound of the falling rain. It is also by inclusion of the elements that nature exceeds the mere sum of sensible things.

There remains still the question as to whether, granted these moments of excess, the extent of nature is to be limited or whether nature is to be determined as including all that is, hence as coextensive with being. Would it be possible, for the sake of accord with what Emerson calls the common sense of nature, to distinguish it from the cosmos at large? Could such a distinction be drawn without simply reinstating in another guise the Ptolemaic distinction—long since refuted—between the sublunary world and the incorruptible heaven? One possibility would be to regard the sky as the limit separating nature from the cosmos, for, like any genuine limit, the sky displays a peculiar relation to each of the regions it would distinguish. From within nature and to the senses naturally employed, the sky appears as a uniform dome that, together with the earth, encloses the enchorial space in which the things that concern humans come to pass. But when the senses are supplemented, as by powerful telescopes, so that humans can look beyond the surface appearance that is the sky, the sky as such dissolves and becomes an opening onto the cosmos.

If such a distinction between nature and cosmos were to be elaborated, then while extraterrestrial entities such as black holes would be regarded as beyond nature, they could nonetheless be taken as attesting to the limit of the sensible. For such entities do not present themselves to the senses. If, in the wake of the Nietzschean inversion, there is presentation *only* to the senses, then it follows that such entities do not present themselves at all. Recognition of such entities would require, then, that the very sense of being as presence be suspended.

27. See the more extensive discussion below in chap. 5; also my *Force of Imagination: The Sense of the Elemental* (Bloomington: Indiana University Press, 2000), chap. 6.

Yet within nature, presence would remain decisive, at least in connection with the elements. It is in this regard that one could begin to elaborate a sense of the imperative beyond the range of the Nietzschean inversion. For, quite apart from theoretical reflections on nature, humans share a capacity to be entranced by elemental nature. When we stand motionless and silent with our gaze fixed upon a towering mountain peak or an expanse of sea stretching to the horizon, our interest is neither in seeing what a mountain or sea looks like nor in coming to know what its essence is. Rather, standing in the presence of the elemental, we simply abide with it and let our senses be absorbed by it. In giving ourselves over to it, we at the same time enhance our sense of belonging to the elemental—in a sense of sense irreducible to mere perception and to essential cognition. By engaging such an elemental sense, a path can perhaps be opened for rethinking the return to nature in a manner that, at once, advances beyond mere inversion while also returning to the beginnings of Western philosophy.

4 RETURN FROM THE NATURE BEYOND NATURE

There is a certain Platonism that sets nature apart. It is not the Platonism of the dialogues, if indeed the disclosures achieved through the words, deeds, and myths of the dialogues can, in any coherent sense, be designated as Platonism. Rather, it is a Platonism that is set in position, that has undergone a transformation into a position that is placed in opposition to others. It becomes possible to trace the stages by which, in the history of metaphysics, this position comes to be dismantled. Indeed, it is precisely at the point where the dismantling has been carried through to completion, where the position has unraveled entirely, and where its constituent moments are again set in motion, that Nietzsche, from this point, undertakes to trace this history from beginning to end.

This alleged Platonism takes as a clue the double meaning of *nature* and extends it to the limit in both possible directions. On the one hand, there is nature as it is displayed before our senses, the nature that consists of mountains and rivers, trees and flowers. At the limit—the lower limit—nature in this sense is reduced to mere sensation, to the disordered and fleeting colors, sounds, etc., that are received through the senses. Yet, what remains after this reduction is no longer the nature that consists of mountains and rivers, trees and flowers. In order that it be reconstituted as nature, determinacy must supervene upon it from elsewhere, from somewhere beyond nature, a somewhere that, almost paradoxically, is also nowhere, since it is not to be found anywhere within nature in its spatial expanse. The position that is forged (in both senses) thus posits a nature beyond nature; it is, then, from this beyond that nature would receive the determinacy by which it becomes the nature consisting of mountains and rivers, trees and flowers. This nature beyond nature would constitute the very sense, the meaning, the essence of nature. Apart from nature in its sensible presence, this nature beyond nature would itself be distinguished as intelligible.

It is Nietzsche who confronted most directly the alleged Platonism that issued in these results. On the other hand, Platonism never ceased to be a provocation for Nietzsche. Never, despite all the gestures to the contrary, was Platonism forced to settle into a well-defined form and thus brought fully under control. Never is it consigned once and for all to a preordained place in the history of thought in such a way as to guarantee that it will not return to haunt thinking in the very turn to another beginning. While expressing his deep mistrust of Plato, branding him as an aberration from the basic instincts of the Greeks, as pre-existently Christian, Nietzsche describes him, at the opposite extreme, as an artist who preferred appearance (*Schein*) to being.[1]

Nonetheless, Platonism most often assumes for Nietzsche the guise of a position to be overcome. In particular, this overcoming is to be an overturning, an inverting, of Platonism. This figure of inversion remains effective throughout the entire course of Nietzsche's thought, from the time of *The Birth of Tragedy* up through his final creative year. It is already explicit in one of the sketches made as Nietzsche was preparing *The Birth of Tragedy*. In the sketch he writes: "My philosophy an *inverted Platonism*: the further removed from true being, the purer, the more beautiful, the better it is. Living in *Schein* as goal."[2] There is perhaps no other passage that anticipates so perfectly and at such an early date the inversion that will come more and more to structure Nietzsche's thought as a whole. In particular, it is evident already at this very early stage how Nietzsche's thought will come to bear on the determination of nature, how it will revoke the positing of nature beyond nature, how it will initiate a return of nature from the beyond of nature.

The terms of the Nietzschean inversion are first taken up thematically in the initial volume of *Human, All Too Human*, published in 1878. What in the early sketch was called "true being" is now designated as "the metaphysical world," this designation serving as the title of the aphorism addressed to this theme. Nietzsche begins with what has the appearance of a concession: "It is true, there could be a metaphysical world; the absolute possibility of it is hardly to be disputed." This possibility is,

---

1. On Nietzsche's relation to Platonism, see my *Platonic Legacies* (Albany: State University of New York Press, 2004), chap. 1.

2. Friedrich Nietzsche, *Nachgelassene Fragmente: Herbst 1869–Herbst 1872*, vol. III/3 of *Werke: Kritische Gesamtausgabe* (Berlin: Walter de Gruyter, 1977), 207 (7 [156]).

however, of the emptiest, most abstract sort, and Nietzsche characterizes it as "a purely scientific problem," one not likely to be much of a bother to anyone. But then, with a sudden injection of genealogy, Nietzsche completely recasts the problem; for what he declares to lie behind the belief in metaphysical assumptions, prompting this belief, begetting these assumptions, is passion, error, and self-deception. He concludes: "When one has disclosed these methods"—in effect, these non-methods—"as the foundation of all extant religions and metaphysical systems, one has refuted them!" Nietzsche grants that even after this refutation the empty possibility of a metaphysical world remains; and yet, he adds, "one can do absolutely nothing with it, not to speak of letting happiness, salvation, and life depend on the spiderwebs of such a possibility." Nothing could even be said of this world except that it is other, that it is inaccessible and incomprehensible. Even if, against all likelihood, the existence of such a world could somehow be demonstrated and if knowledge could be had of it, this knowledge would be utterly useless, even more useless than knowledge of the chemical composition of water would be to a sailor endangered by a storm at sea. Short of such a most unlikely demonstration, there is nothing to motivate positing such a metaphysical world as existing, granted that the passion and lies that otherwise supported it have been exposed as such.[3]

In this aphorism a shift is detectable, a shift from the metaphysical world in general to the thing-in-itself specifically. Another aphorism,[4] entitled "Appearance and Thing-in-itself," stages the problem dramatically. Philosophers are portrayed as stationing themselves before the so-called world of appearance as though it were a painting depicting a scene; their task is to interpret this scene so as to draw a conclusion about the nature of the thing-in-itself, which is regarded as the ground of this world. While some venture such conclusions, other philosophers contend that there is no connection, that from the world of appearance no conclusion can be drawn regarding the thing-in-itself. Against both parties, against both those who affirm and those who deny such a connection, Nietzsche poses another alternative: that the character of the world of appearances has, in its becoming, been determined, not by the thing-in-itself, but by a human, all too human process. Here is how Nietzsche describes it: "Because we have for millennia made moral, aesthetic, religious claims, looked upon the world with blind desire,

---

3. Nietzsche, *Menschliches, Allzumenschliches I*, in vol. IV/2 of *Werke*, 25f. (§9).
4. Ibid., 32–34 (§16).

passion, or fear, and abandoned ourselves to the bad habits of illogical thinking, this world has gradually *become* so wondrously variegated, frightful, meaningful, soulful, it has acquired color—but we have been the colorists: it is the human intellect that has let appearance appear and transported [*hineingetragen*] its erroneous basic conceptions into things." Thus, just as, according to the earlier aphorism, passion and lies produced the metaphysical world and thus the thing-in-itself, so likewise it is human desire, passion, and misconception that have colored the world of appearance, that have brought it to appear as it does. And yet, exposing the true nature of such appearance requires that the appearing be interrupted; it requires, says Nietzsche, a rigorous science (*strenge Wissenschaft*) capable of detaching us, a discipline that can "lift us up out of the entire process." It is no doubt in aiming at such detachment from the human, all too human process of appearing that the book *Human, All Too Human* is, as its subtitle declares, a book for free spirits.

These analyses bear significantly on the inversion of Platonism at which Nietzsche aims. The metaphysical world—in Platonic terms, the intelligible, τὸ νοητόν—is shown to be so vacuous, so innocuous, so utterly irrelevant, that even if it were to remain as an empty possibility, the full weight of what is called reality would still be shifted to the world of appearance. Hence, the inversion would in effect be carried out, primacy now being given to—in Platonic terms—the sensible, τὸ αἰσθητόν, while the intelligible becomes, at most, only secondary. Furthermore, with this inversion, the terms themselves do not go unaltered, do not merely exchange places in the schema, the lower becoming the higher, and conversely. Not only does the alleged ground of being get reconstrued as empty possibility, but also the world of appearance, previously construed in relation to this ground, is now referred instead to the genealogy of subjectivity, to the human, all too human process by which misconceptions are carried over into things so as to appear—or reappear—as the character of the things.

Nature is thus recalled to nature. Rather than being determined by a nature beyond nature, by an intelligibility that would impose determinacy upon nature, such determinacy would now be taken to have its source in subjectivity. In place of the metaphysical ground of nature, Nietzsche substitutes a subjective ground. Thus, nature is not freed of determination from and by an origin set apart. It is simply that this determining origin is now taken to be located elsewhere.

A brief account has been given already of the way in which the figure of the inversion of Platonism remains operative in Nietzsche's writings in the 1880s, especially in *Twilight of the Idols*.[5] That account needs to be supplemented by four additional points.

First of all, it should be noted that a remarkable feature of *Twilight of the Idols* lies in its use of modifying punctuation, quotation marks set around certain words in order to indicate a double meaning, or rather a shift from the traditional sense to its effacement and replacement, this shift corresponding precisely to the inversion of Platonism that the text effects. Thus, when Nietzsche writes of reason in philosophy, using this phrase as a section title,[6] he sets the word *reason* in quotation marks so as to represent graphically what the text itself declares: that what has been called by this name, what has been taken as reason, is now exposed as a power of dissimulation that has led us to falsify the testimony of the senses and to add to the apparent world the lie of a true world. The name of this true world that has been exposed as a lie, the expression "true world," thus also appears in quotation marks. Even in writing that "the 'apparent' world is the only one," such modifying or doubling punctuation must come to mark the word *apparent* (*scheinbare*); for as soon as it is recognized as the only world (*die einzige*), the designation of it as apparent begins to lose its appropriateness, and it becomes necessary to mark a shift, a certain effacement, of the designation. In these as well as numerous other passages, Nietzsche proves to be a superb master of punctuation.

Attention should be drawn, secondly, to the way in which the figure of the inversion of Platonism is presented in its most concentrated form in the section of *Twilight of the Idols* entitled "How the 'True World' Finally Became a Fable." Here, in barely more than one page, Nietzsche recounts the history of philosophy precisely as the series of positions by which the inversion of Platonism has come about. Beginning with the true world of Plato—*true world* written without quotation marks—Nietzsche tells of the six stages by which this true world—acquiring quotation marks in the course of the story—finally came to be exposed as an error, how its history, the history told here, proved to be, as the section subtitle says, the history of an error.

In this story the penultimate stage is that of the pandemonium (*Teufelslärm*) of all free spirits, thus the stage enacted in *Human, All Too Human* where the "true world"—with quotation marks—proves useless,

---

5. See chap. 3 above.
6. Nietzsche, *Götzen-Dämmerung*, in vol. VI/3 of *Werke*, 68–73. The subtitle of the work is *Wie man mit dem Hammer philosophirt*.

superfluous, and so is to be abolished. Then, in writing of the final stage, the stage that this very text enacts, Nietzsche says: "The true world we have abolished: what world has remained? The apparent one, perhaps? ... But no! *With the true world we have also abolished the apparent one!*"[7]

This enactment, the completion of the inversion of Platonism, Nietzsche marks as noon, the moment of the shortest shadow. It is the moment of escape from the long shadow cast by Platonism, the moment of liberation that comes only with the end of this longest error. It is also the moment of dissolution in which the future becomes sheer possibility, the opening of a new era for mankind (*Menschheit*), indeed the high point of mankind opening beyond mankind. It is the moment in which the stage is set for Zarathustra's first speech to the people, the speech that begins: "*I teach you the overman.* Man is something that is to be overcome."[8] It is a moment that Nietzsche thus marks with the indication: INCIPIT ZARATHUSTRA.

But then, thirdly, what remains once the inversion has been carried through? In a sense nothing remains. The true world has been abolished, and now the apparent world also is abolished, is recognized as having already been abolished with the abolition of the true world. Nothing remains, neither the intelligible, metaphysical world nor the apparent, sensible world. Yet the sense of the abolition is not the same in both cases. The intelligible world is abolished in the sense that it is no longer regarded as existing, is no longer accorded even the empty possibility that was still granted it in *Human, All Too Human*. It is this abolition that is expressed when Zarathustra, just before coming to speak for the first time to the people, muses that perhaps the old hermit he has met in the forest has not yet heard that God is dead. What is said here in terms of Christianity—identified by Nietzsche as "Platonism for the people"[9]—means that the intelligible world has vanished with an absoluteness comparable to that of death.

Yet, this is, most decidedly, not the sense in which the sensible world has been abolished. What has been abolished is the character of the apparent, that is, appearing, world *as* apparent, as the appearance of a true world beyond. Thus, the effect of the inversion of Platonism, once it is fully carried out to the point of this final abolition, is neither

---

7. Ibid., 75. The ellipsis occurs in Nietzsche's text.
8. Nietzsche, *Also Sprach Zarathustra*, in vol. VI/1 of *Werke*, 8.
9. "Christenthum ist Platonismus für's 'Volk'" (*Jenseits von Gut und Böse*, in vol. VI/2 of *Werke*, 4).

simply to invert the terms nor even, once they are inverted, to institute a new hierarchy, a new ordering structure. Fully and decisively twisting free of Platonism—to use David Krell's wonderful translation of *Herausdrehung*—requires letting go of the intelligible world and hence of all ordering of it with respect to the sensible. The effect of the inversion of Platonism is to constrain thinking entirely to the sensible and thus finally to efface its very character as inversion.

What, finally, does the inversion entail as regards the determination of nature? As belonging to the sensible, indeed as virtually identical with the sensible, nature too is freed from determination from beyond. It can no longer be regarded as receiving its determination from an intelligible origin set apart from it. No longer can it be supposed that nature, reduced to mere sensation, becomes truly nature, becomes the nature consisting of mountains and rivers, trees and flowers, only through determination from beyond, from what would constitute the very essence of nature. Once the inversion is carried through to the point where it effaces itself, nature is given back to itself. Carried through to this point, the inversion issues in a return of nature from the beyond, a return of nature from the nature of nature, from what has been, but no longer can be, taken as the nature of nature.

Once it is recognized that the Nietzschean inversion abolishes not only the intelligible ground of sensible, natural things but also the subjective ground that Nietzsche posits, then it becomes evident that such things must be interrogated in quite another way than that found especially in Nietzsche's earlier works. Once it is recognized that recourse to subjectivity in order to account for the determinacy of such things is no less metaphysical than recourse to the intelligible, then the imperative is that they must be understood *from themselves*. To understand them from themselves requires, in turn, that they be apprehended as they show themselves or as they can be brought to show themselves; and it requires that thinking bind itself to the self-showing of things. While it is perhaps phenomenology that has made this imperative most explicit, it is an imperative that is repeatedly resumed and renewed throughout the history of philosophy from Plato on.[10] To take up this imperative and to bind thinking to it is to renew once again one of the most profound motifs in the history of philosophy.

---

10. See my discussion under the title "The Identities of the Things Themselves," chap. 16 of *Delimitations: Phenomenology and the End of Metaphysics*, 2nd ed. (Bloomington: Indiana University Press, 1995).

If, in this connection, sensible things can still be called appearances, what this designates is their own appearing, their own self-showing, not that they serve for the appearing of something else that exceeds the world of appearance. Yet, such a renewal cannot simply pass over the basic difference between what Nietzsche declares regarding appearances and what would be envisioned in this imperative. For, according to the analysis in *Human, All Too Human*, appearances, though not determined by things-in-themselves, are determined by a human, all too human process. Things appear as they do because we have colored them, because, in more rigorous terms, we—here the "we" means: the genesis of subjectivity—carry misconceptions over to things, transport them there in such a way that they then reappear as characters of the appearing things. Thus, according to this analysis, things do not show themselves *as themselves* but rather as having a character, a coloring, that has been transported to them from and by subjectivity.

And yet, this very analysis demonstrates in deed, in its being carried out, that it is possible for us to interrupt such appearing and thereby to disengage from it those characters that have their source in subjectivity rather than in the things themselves. As noted already, Nietzsche even alludes to the rigorous science that, detaching us from the process, would make it possible to disengage those apparent characters that, alien to the things themselves, only distort, falsify, conceal the things. Such rigorous science could be conceived as carrying out a series of reductions aimed at bringing the things themselves to show themselves as themselves.

Suppose, then, a thinking that would take up the inversion of Platonism and carry it through. It might readily be assumed that such thinking would have as its task peeling away, as it were, the layers of misconceptions covering the things themselves; thereby the things would be freed from everything subjective and brought to stand forth in what could properly be called their pure, transparent objectivity. And yet, matters are not nearly so simple, nor the task manifestly so straightforward. In particular, this assumption overlooks two crucial considerations, two possibilities that pose complications, the consequences of which are virtually unlimited.

The first consideration is that even if everything subjectively imposed upon things could be disengaged and set apart, there would still be no necessity that things show themselves transparently, that they come fully to light as themselves. While they would indeed show themselves as themselves and from themselves, there remains the possibility that things also offer resistance to showing themselves, that in that very showing they also withhold themselves. Indeed, the most elementary circumstance of perception offers support for this possibility: that in the perception of an object, one has present to one's vision only certain faces of the object, while others remain unseen. In the Preface to *The Gay Science*, Nietzsche puts it more dramatically: "We no longer believe that truth remains truth when the veils are withdrawn from it.... Today we consider it a matter of decency not to wish to see everything naked."[11]

The second consideration is that the process of transporting subjective conceptions into the object may, if properly conceived, prove to be not an obstacle to but rather a primary moment in the self-showing of things. To develop this possibility requires that subjectivity be displaced and that the process of letting certain conceptions appear to frame things be rethought as the very opening of the space of manifestation. It is a matter of rethinking the process, no longer as a transporting of subjective into objective, but as the way in which we, by our relation to the space in which things show themselves, contribute to letting self-showing as such take place.[12]

In any case, for a thinking that would follow through the inversion of Platonism, the imperative remains that sensible things be understood from themselves and not as mere images of alleged intelligibles. Thus, whatever the complications and whatever possibilities must at least be left open to further consideration, what is required is a new interpretation of the sensible. This interpretation must be such that the sensible is understood neither through its opposition to the intelligible nor through recourse to subjectivity but from itself, that is, as it unfolds before the senses and for an apprehension geared to the senses. Nature is to be understood from itself; it is to be returned to itself.

Nietzsche took a first step in this direction, drawing the consequences of the inversion of Platonism out toward a new beginning. In certain of his texts and fragments from the mid- and late 1880s, the outline of a new interpretation of the sensible can be discerned. This interpretation can be summed up in two words: The first of these is *perspective* or *perspectival*. In the preface to *Beyond Good and Evil*, dated 1885, Nietzsche links the question of perspective directly with Platonism. He refers to Plato's invention of the pure spirit and the good

---

11. Nietzsche, *Die fröhliche Wissenschaft*, in vol. V/2 of *Werke*, 20.
12. I am referring here to the analysis in *Force of Imagination*, esp. 197–99.

as such, characterizing it as "the most dangerous of all errors so far" and celebrating both the fact that this error is now overcome and that we—presumably the free spirits of the time—are heirs to the strength gained in the long struggle against this error. Then he identifies the fundamental error that was at the core of Plato's invention of pure spirit and the good: "To be sure, it meant standing truth on its head and denying the *perspectival*, the basic condition of all life, to speak of spirit and the good as Plato did."[13] The figure coheres perfectly with that of the inversion of Platonism: to invert Platonism, now that this error is overcome, amounts to standing truth back on its feet and affirming the perspectival as the basic condition of life.

In a fragment from early 1888, Nietzsche explains precisely how the moment of perspective, of the perspectival, belongs constitutively to the sensible, to the apparent world (*die scheinbare Welt*), as he calls it both in the fragment and in the contemporaneous text *Twilight of the Idols*. According to Nietzsche's account, the apparent world is the world as seen from the viewpoint of utility in the preservation and enhancement of the power of a certain species of animal. As Nietzsche expresses it, more generally: "Every center of force adopts a perspective toward the entire remainder." It is this viewpoint, this perspective, that determines how the world appears. Nietzsche writes: "The perspective therefore decides the character of the 'apparentness' [*giebt den Charakter der 'Scheinbarkeit' ab*]!"[14] Furthermore, Nietzsche insists that it is not as though a world would remain intact if one deducted the perspective, not as though the perspectival character of the world were a mere overlay that could be removed. Rather, this perspectival character belongs constitutively to the sensible, determining how it appears as such.

The second of the two words that sum up Nietzsche's new interpretation of the sensible is *Schein*. If, in hopes of retaining somewhat the unity of the word, we translate it as *shining*, it is imperative to bear in mind the broad range of senses the word commands: shining, shine, appearance, semblance, illusion. Equally important is its affinity with *Erscheinung* (appearance—less ambiguously) and with *scheinbar* (apparent), as in *die scheinbare Welt* (the apparent world). Although Nietzsche grants that *Erscheinung* is one of those "fateful words that appear to

---

13. Nietzsche, *Jenseits von Gut und Böse*, in vol. VI/2 of *Werke*, 4.
14. Nietzsche, *Nachgelassene Fragmente: Anfang 1888 bis Anfang Januar 1889*, vol. VIII/3 of *Werke*, 162f. (14 [184]).

express knowledge but that in truth hinder it,"[15] the fact remains that in *The Birth of Tragedy*, specifically in the analysis of the Apollinian, Nietzsche went quite far toward renewing the polysemic force of the word *Schein*.[16]

It is only in a few late fragments that Nietzsche gives some positive indications as to how shining belongs to the character of the sensible. In every case Nietzsche's intent is to undercut the usual distinction between reality and shining, that is, between the reality that would belong to things as such and the shining forth by which they would appear, by which they would become apparent. Over against this distinction, this simple opposition, Nietzsche maintains that the character of apparentness belongs to the very reality of things. Thus, in a fragment from early 1888, which begins by dismissing the so-called true—as opposed to apparent—world as a mere fiction, Nietzsche continues: "Apparentness [*Scheinbarkeit*] itself belongs to reality: it is a form of its being, that is, in a world where there is no being, a certain calculable world of *identical* cases must first be created through *shining*."[17] In other words, since there is no being, there is only appearing; or rather, appearing is the being of things, the way in which they *are*. Because things are not simply present, because they would not remain intact after the deduction of the perspectives in which they appear, their very occurrence must be their appearing, their shining forth in such a way as to become apparent. Because they are nothing beyond their perspectives, they are nothing outside their shining appearance.

Thus, in another fragment, dated 1885, Nietzsche is explicit about the identification of shining with reality. He writes: "Shining as I understand it is the actual and sole reality of things." It is not as though things simply were—or could be—without shining and appearing; rather, they *are*—they are real—only as shining forth so as to appear. Hence, Nietzsche continues: "Thus I do not posit 'shining' in opposition to 'reality'

---

15. Nietzsche, *Nachgelassene Fragmente: Herbst 1884–Herbst 1885*, vol. VII/3 of *Werke*, 386 (40 [52]). Heidegger raises doubts as to whether Nietzsche became "master of the fate entrenched in that word" (Heidegger, *Nietzsche* [Pfullingen: Günther Neske, 1961], 1:248). There is a discrepancy between the passage as Heidegger cites it and as it is given in the Colli-Montinari edition: in the former, two examples of such words are given, *Schein* and *Erscheinung*, whereas in the latter only *Erscheinung* is given.

16. See my discussion in *Crossings: Nietzsche and the Space of Tragedy* (Chicago: University of Chicago Press, 1991), chap. 1.

17. Nietzsche, *Nachgelassene Fragmente: Anfang 1888 bis Anfang Januar 1889*, vol. VIII/3 of *Werke*, 62f. (14 [93]).

but on the contrary take shining as the reality that resists transformation into an imaginative 'world of truth.'"[18] Shining is the very reality of things, and it is their shining, rather than some inert state of being, that bestows on them their resistance, their resistance to being transformed into something merely imagined (so, reality in distinction from phantasy) and their resistance to being assimilated, as in Platonism, to an alleged true world. Rather, as they shine forth in their perspectives, things persist in their apparentness, in their sensibleness.

In Nietzsche's interpretation of the sensible as perspectival shining, as shining in perspective, the proximity of his thought to more recent thought is evident. To establish this connection would require that the human, all too human process by which, according to Nietzsche, subjectivity transports conceptions into the object be interrogated in a more rigorous way. Yet, in referring to the rigorous science that could lift us up out of the entire process, Nietzsche acknowledges—as the coherence of his own text requires—the possibility of a rigorous analysis of this process and, above all, of the concepts that Nietzsche's account of it takes for granted, most notably, those of subject and object. The introduction, for instance, of the concept of intentionality would have profound and indeed subversive consequences for the transpositional schema that Nietzsche takes to be operative. This concept and its phenomenological elaboration would allow a precise differentiation to be established between a perceptually engaged act of consciousness, capable of intuitive fulfillment, and an act of phantasy in which consciousness would bring something before itself in a way that could not be fulfilled in sense intuition.

Yet clearly Nietzsche's conception of the perspectival character of appearances, if detached from his residual metaphysics of force and then developed in a more descriptive manner, leads directly to the problematic of horizonality. Most notably—though not by any means exclusively—this character links up with what can be designated as the lateral horizon. By this is meant the ordered totality of other profiles or faces of an object that is cointended when an object is—as always—seen from a particular perspective. The task is, then, to render a descriptive account of just how it is that objects, appearing to a particular perspective, show themselves within a lateral horizon, which bestows on them the depth and density of the real.

18. Nietzsche, *Nachgelassene Fragmente: Herbst 1884–Herbst 1885*, vol. VII/3 of *Werke*, 386 (40 [53]).

As to shining, Nietzsche's account would need to be taken much further toward differentiating between shining (*Schein*) and appearing (*Erscheinung*). In the fragments cited, the character of shining expresses for the most part simply the apparent character of things, the fact that they occur only in appearing. Thus, in Nietzsche's account, shining is not determined as a positive character belonging to the appearing or, more precisely, to the self-showing of things. In the one passage in the fragments where Nietzsche does propose a determinate name meant to characterize reality, that is, shining, from within, he resorts to saying that it is will to power.[19] If, on the other hand, one insists on stopping short of the metaphysics of the will to power, if, instead of installing the will to power as an inner core of things withdrawn from their appearing, one persists—more insistently than Nietzsche himself—with the identification of reality with appearing, then one will need to ask about the character that, within appearing, shining assumes. What, one must ask, must be the character of shining such that things can come to show themselves precisely by shining in perspective, by shining within the complex of horizons that belong to the scene of self-showing? What does it mean to shine? Or is shining an occurrence so delicate that it escapes—or appears to escape—meaning? As the brilliant red of a male cardinal, seen across a woodland path, shines against the glistening snow. Even as, with a drastic reduction of horizons, a natural reduction, the deep blue of a cloudless sky shines forth in a manner so singular that it seems to escape, to exceed, even the word with which we would pretend to name it.

---

19. "A determinate name for this reality would be 'the will to power,' namely, designated from within and not in terms of its ungraspable, flowing Prometheus-nature" (ibid.). The contrast with sheer becoming serves to reveal that in effect Nietzsche is simply installing being (by another name) behind the appearing, behind the shining in perspective.

5 THE ELEMENTAL TURN

A turn will become imperative, a turn to nature, to the natural elements. It will be required most directly and most urgently, not by theoretical exigencies, but by the necessity of confronting, in word and action, the devastation to which nature is increasingly exposed, devastation that has now assumed such gigantic proportions that the life-sustaining capacity of the earth itself is threatened. Already foreseen by the most farsighted thinkers as the turn began to be enacted from the heroism of the mastery of nature to the advocacy of ecological restraint, the assault on nature has now been mounted on a scale that could hardly have been envisaged a few decades ago. Driven not just by technology but at a deeper level by political and economic interests, this assault has produced a situation for which the word *crisis*—even if heightened by multiple superlatives—is an extreme understatement.

It is a situation that calls for new insight and concerted action. Yet if these responses are truly to bear on all that is at stake, they must avoid replicating, in their aim and their strategy, the very comportment to nature that has led to the present impasse. Simply to propose to control technological development, to limit its application, to bring it under human mastery, is to repeat at another level the strategy by which technology itself brings nature under its control. To propose to master the political is even more repetitive; such a venture recoils on itself, since the task of controlling the political could only be carried out by political means, thus employing the very constellation of forces that it would seek to displace. On the other hand, the incapacity, in both the technological and the political spheres, to address successfully the assault on nature must not be used to support a retreat into quietism nor a repose in which one would wait for an unforeseeable event capable of providing deliverance from the advance of technology—if for no other reason than that the assault would in the meanwhile gain ever greater ascendancy. What must intervene is theoretical reflection capable of setting its sights upon nature in another way, in a way that is more attuned to the natural elements themselves and that attests to this attunement.

Thus, a turn to nature will become imperative for philosophy; or rather, it has already become imperative and will only become ever more urgently so. This turn will be a return, for in the course of its history, philosophy has repeatedly undertaken to return to nature, to catch sight again of elements of nature that had been obscured through adherence to the artifices of custom, to the excesses of theologically motivated thought, or to the hegemony of economic processes. Yet the return to nature that is now to become ever more imperative is one that must span the entire course on which philosophy has previously carried out the turn to nature. Returning to the point where the turn away from nature is first ventured, philosophy will be called on to dismantle the frame of this turn so as to return to a nature that, since the beginning of philosophy, has seldom been thought, that, except in the beginning, has perhaps never been thought. Philosophy will become—though differently, very differently—what it was in the beginning. Where will it come to be? It will return to the beginning, will station itself in proximity to the beginning.

The philosophical turn to nature is a return in still another sense. For, before philosophical thought commences, we are always already turned toward nature, thoroughly engaged with it from the moment we draw our first breath, walking upon the earth and depending on the stability it offers to us and to the shelters we build on it, shelters that protect us from the natural elements to which we are exposed, from the rain, the wind, the snow. We are engaged also—though in a very different way—with the sky. From the sky come rain and snow, driven by the wind, which attests to the air that spreads from the earth up toward the sky. From the sky comes much of what is necessary for life; it is from the sky that sunlight spreads across the earth illuminating the things and elements that belong to the earth, rendering them visible to us. Even in the most artificial settings where we succeed in replicating the stability of the earth and the light of the sun, we continue to depend on nature for the very sustenance of life, for food, water, air, and so on.

Thus, the philosophical turn to nature is necessarily a return to that to which, as the very condition of life, we are already turned. It is a return in search of insight into nature itself, into what is proper to nature, into what determines it as nature, into that which, in the most proper sense, is nature as such, or, letting the double meaning of the word come into play, into the nature of nature.

The character and necessity of this return have been clarified through the various reflections assembled around the injunction "*zur Sache selbst*," though what phenomenology is enjoined thereby to take as its object is not limited to nature. In fact, in the course of its development, phenomenology has come to put in question the identity of the pertinent *Sache* and has carried out multiple, diverse determinations of just what it is.[1] Furthermore, it has increasingly come to light that this injunction is by no means unique to twentieth-century phenomenology. It can be heard already in Empedocles' instruction to his pupil Pausanias that he is to consider all things in the way in which they are manifest (δῆλον). It resounds in Plato's appeal to τὸ πρᾶγμα αὐτό (in the Seventh Letter) and in Hegel's insistence on attending to the *Sache* and on being guided entirely by it. The turn to the *Sache* that twentieth-century phenomenology proposes to undertake is to this extent a renewal of a move ventured repeatedly in the history of philosophy. Phenomenology radicalizes the turn, makes the bond to the *Sache* its principle of principles, regardless of how the identity of the *Sache* is determined. Its adherence to the *Sache* is precisely what constitutes its rigor.

Yet if today, in what borders on post-phenomenological thought, there is a certain solidarity with the Greek beginning, it is because in the turn to nature the *Sache* has proved to involve the elements in a sense akin to the way they were thought by the early Greek thinkers. More precisely, such thought proposes to distinguish between natural things and the elements of nature and construes the elements in their specific character as elemental. In addition, it will be necessary to take up the classical distinction between intelligible and sensible and to take distance from this distinction in the form in which, heedless of all the questions, reservations, even comedies about it that abound in the Platonic dialogues, it was passed down in the history of philosophy and rendered entirely unproblematic. In this form it becomes a distinction posited between an intelligible or supersensible beyond and nature in its sensible presence. It is this form of the distinction that must now be

---

1. See my discussion in "The Identities of the Things Themselves," chap. 16 of *Delimitations*.

dismantled, thereby inhibiting the turn from nature to a kind of nature beyond nature.² Having thus dismantled the very frame of the classical turn, this thought to come will shift its focus to the elemental in its distinction from—and its relation to—natural things. The ancient order of intelligible and sensible (νοητόν καὶ αἰσθητόν) will be replaced by the dyad of elements and things.

But what is an elemental? How is it that what were called elements (στοιχεῖα) are to be thought as elemental? What is the sense of elemental, and how are elementals related to sense as such? Furthermore, how is it possible even to pose these questions in a rigorous way, especially as questions that ask about the *what*? For to give a rigorous sense to such questions will require, in the end, construing them as asking about an εἶδος, about an intelligible idea, thus reinscribing the question within the frame of the very distinction that, having been dismantled, would be surpassed. The only alternative is to defer rigorously formulating the question in order, first of all, as preparation, to build up a discourse on the elementals that shies away from such entrapments by attending in a more descriptive idiom to the elements as they are—or can become—manifest.

The most comprehensive of the elementals are earth and sky. These delimit the space in which natural things come to pass and become manifest. It can appropriately be called enchorial space in order to indicate that it represents a way of rethinking what in the *Timaeus* was called, among other names (none of which were simply names), the χώρα. It is within the χώρα that the elements are situated, even when they are not yet quite themselves and, if more remotely, once they have taken shape. In a sense it can be regarded as a kind of space before space, at least insofar as all other spaces, including those occupied by natural things and even those to which certain elements are attached, are limitations of the χώρα.³ It is likewise when the χώρα is rethought as enchorial space. Such space has only the most indefinite limits, as it extends up toward the most indefinite of all the elements, the sky. And, like the χώρα, it precedes the delimitations by which, for example, the isotropic spaces of geometry are given form.

---

2. See the discussion above in chap. 4.
3. I have given an extensive account of the discourse on the χώρα found in the *Timaeus*. See *Chorology*, chap. 3.

While earth and sky do not show themselves as natural or sensible things, they also do not belong to a domain other than and apart from the natural and the sensible. They show themselves as being *of* the sensible without being themselves sensible things. While they belong to nature and grant natural things an expanse in which to appear, they show themselves to be manifestly irreducible to mere natural things.

Yet how is it that the elements are differentiated from things? In what ways are earth and sky, sea and forest, wind and rain, thunder and lightning other than things? What is it about them and about their way of being manifest to us that distinguishes them from things?

On the one hand, we are surrounded by things, by discrete, individually delimited things, but also by things that coalesce in such a way as not to be simply individualized. In every case we comport ourselves to things across a certain distinct interval. On the other hand, we are encompassed by elementals, which, as encompassing, are less readily objectifiable and less distinctly individualized. This character is perhaps most striking when we find ourselves in the midst of a thunderstorm. In a high mountain valley, for instance, the dark clouds will advance up the valley until they cover it entirely so that it is completely encompassed by the storm that follows. Along with all other animate creatures, we will be encompassed by the storm so unconditionally that it cannot be escaped but must be endured by finding the best shelter available. The wind will sweep through the valley, bringing with it the driving rain, both wind and rain encompassing the entire landscape. A flash of lightning will spread its illumination across the sky and light up the valley across its full breadth. Thunder will echo from the mountains so as to give a certain measure of their contours as they rise on both sides of the valley, their peaks exposing the earth to heights otherwise improper to it. In the storm all these elements are gathered, and while each encompasses the landscape in its particular way, they also intersect, overlap, and envelop one another. The storm is precisely this running-together, this concurrence, of the elements and of their various encompassings.

No other elemental is as openly encompassing as the sky. Its character as encompassing is the most open, the most manifest, because, in most places outside the enclosures we construct, virtually the entire dome of the sky can be seen. In this regard it stands in contrast to the earth, which, though it can be conceived as no less encompassing than the sky, is not openly so, for we never see more than a small parcel of land, not even from the panorama afforded by mountain peaks. Even on the open sea, the visible expanse, even if stretching to the horizon, does not quite match the open encompassing of the sky.

Elementals are also distinguished from things in that they are not determinately bounded in the way that things, even the least individualized things, are. Though of course the storm is not simply unlimited in its extent, it is sufficiently indefinite that one cannot readily say just how far it extends; even if it is regarded meteorologically—and thus in a way that begins to level out the very difference at issue—there remains at least a trace of this indefiniteness. The indefiniteness of elementals is linked to another character that they display: elementals are gigantic, if not simply monstrous, in their extent. For they utterly exceed the proportions of humans and of natural things, indeed in such a way that they share no common measure with the things they encompass.

The expanse of the open sea as it extends to the horizon is indefinite. Not only can one not measure this distance as long as one is at sea, but it makes no sense whatsoever to think of it as extending over a certain distance. If it is truly the open sea, there will, for a very long time, always remain the same expanse, no matter how far one's vessel may sail.

The sky under which all things come to pass is of unlimited extent; its vastness has no measure in common with the things over which it is arched. Yet it does not belong to an order other than the sensible; though distinguished from sensible things, it is nonetheless *of* the sensible. Indeed, its visibility is in a certain respect exemplary. Not only is the sky visible, but also, as the primary region from which light arrives to illuminate things as they come and go, it holds the very source of visibility, bestows that which makes visibility possible and thus, more remotely, is itself a condition of visibility. Furthermore, the sky itself is a *pure visible* both in the sense that it is given to no sense other than vision and in the sense that it is nothing but its visibility, for there is—as we know and despite what we see—no such thing as the sky.

The case of the sky makes it especially evident that elementals are intimately linked to space and time, though they are neither simply spatial nor simply temporal. While the sky arches above all things and, together with the earth, delimits the enchorial space in which things come to pass, and so in this regard is spatial, it is also that from which and by which the time of day and the alternation of day and night are determined. It is from the sky that humans read off—and so first determine—the time. From the sky they receive the measure, most directly of the time of day but also, more extensively, of the time of year and of the passing of the year.

Elementals are also characterized by a peculiar one-sidedness, a one-sidedness that is distinctly different from that displayed by things. Phenomenological analysis has pointed out that, in being perceived, a thing shows at any moment only a single face or profile (*Abschattung*): viewed from the front, it displays one profile, but viewed from the side, it shows another. Yet no matter what the observer's perspective on it might be and no matter which profile it correspondingly displays, that profile will be seen as a profile *of* the thing, as one profile among an indefinite number of others that it would be possible to observe by taking other perspectives on the thing or by turning it about. This ordered set of possible profiles constitutes what is called a lateral horizon. Thus, it turns out that while at any moment the thing displays only a single profile, it shows itself as also harboring in itself a store of other profiles, of other possible views of itself that it could offer. Strictly speaking, then, it is never possible to see simply a single profile, to see one profile alone, for it will always be seen also as a profile of a thing and hence as linked to an entire horizon of other, presently unseen profiles.

With elementals, however, it is otherwise; the very character of their self-showing is different. The side displayed by an elemental—the edge of the wind, for instance—is not a face or a profile behind which a store of others would be harbored. In the case of elementals, the profile that is presented is presented as the only profile—hence as not a profile at all but rather a side that is nonetheless not the side of anything that would have other sides that could be presented. The sky, for instance, has no other side; it makes no sense to suppose that one could see the sky from another perspective. Of course one can observe it under various conditions: at various times of day when the light fills it in different ways and bestows on it various colors, from the radiant blue of midday to the brilliant orange and red of dusk; or on a night when it offers only starlight; or when it is obscured and its light diffused by various kinds and degrees of cloud cover. But, whatever the conditions, one sees always the same face of the sky; one sees it always from the same—the only—perspective. Whatever the conditions under which one sees it, one sees just the sky itself.

In these ways, then, elementals are distinguished from things. Thus different from things, elementals do not accord with the ontological paradigm of thinghood, which has figured prominently in philosophy from Aristotle on. Since they are not things having properties, elementals cannot be accounted for by means of the categories first forged by Aristotle and handed down in various forms throughout the course of philosophy. To the extent that the discipline of logic and even the Western languages themselves are determined by the categories of thinghood, they are not appropriate to the elementals. This is not to say that our logic and language can have no bearing on the elementals; it is not to say that the elementals simply escape, once and for all, being brought to account by use of the logic and the language at our disposal. No phenomenon is simply, unconditionally closed off, not even from a conceptuality based on a structural paradigm at variance with the phenomenon. Still, it is imperative to break with—to break through—the limits of the conceptuality based on thinghood and of the thought and discourse determined by this conceptuality. It is imperative to carry out—to carry through—the turn to the elemental. What is required is a reopening of discourse in which it would cease to be bound to the classical paradigm, a reattuning through which discourse (and the questioning it would both rely on and enable) would be drawn beyond the structures of thinghood and brought into closer accord with the character of the elementals as encompassing, indefinite, gigantic, and peculiarly one-sided. Through such discourse a way would be opened for addressing nature in its elemental bearing and for understanding how the lives of humans—and not only of humans—are both driven and sustained, both exposed and sheltered, by the elements. Through such a turn to the elemental, we will perhaps be enabled to give fitting words to the advocacy of ecological restraint, words that might, in turn, provide directives for action.

Such a reopening of discourse, such a turn to the elemental, will be an imperative for the thinking that is to come. It will be a thinking in which what has been comes to us from out of the future, a thinking in which a return to beginnings coincides with an opening to what is to come.

6 THE COSMOLOGICAL TURN

There are some turns from which there is no turning back. Approaching such a turn, one is not, of course, compelled to press on; the options of retreat or diversion are always available, but only at the cost of consigning oneself to the familiar, well-trodden surroundings. If, however, eschewing such provincialism, one makes the turn and heads across the hitherto unknown landscape, there is no turning back. Never again will things be quite the same.

To be sure, the turn—the most extreme turn—that has now become imperative cannot but reiterate in some measure the turn to nature that philosophy has repeatedly been compelled to carry out: the turn from the polis to the natural universe that occurs when the voice of Timaeus displaces that of Socrates; the turn from society and its inscriptions back to the pure state of nature in search of the origin of human inequality; the turn entailed by the declaration that the whole of modern European philosophy has as its common defect that nature does not exist for it; the imperative that those to come remain true to the earth, the turn, only now foreseen, from the classical hierarchies to the dyad of things and elements. Yet this imperative that imposes itself today demands a turn for which none of these precedents provides a sufficient measure; it requires a turn that would be both more encompassing and also more disruptive in its recoil on philosophical thinking. Let us call it the cosmological turn.

There are occasions—rare, perhaps, but provocative—when something never seen before comes to be seen. There are also occasions when something previously seen only vaguely and indeterminately—a star, for instance, that appears as a mere shimmering point of light—comes to be seen with a clarity and extension sufficient to allow its determination. Such previously unseen or barely seen sights may call for hitherto unthought thoughts. In the most provocative instances, they prompt a turn from which there is no turning back.

In 1572 Tycho Brahe observed the sudden appearance of a new star in the constellation Cassiopeia. The star was extremely bright, so bright that it was visible even during the day. Tycho determined the exact position of the star and compiled a record of its changing brightness from the time of its appearance until, five months later, it faded completely from view. By means of parallax he was able to demonstrate that the distance from the earth to the star was greater than that from the earth to the moon. In other words, the star was shown not to be sublunary.

In 1609 Galileo turned the newly invented telescope heavenward. By means of this instrument he was able to confirm something that was only vaguely evident to unaided perception: that the surface of the moon is not smooth and polished but rather, as Galileo wrote in his treatise *Sidereal Messenger*, is "full of enormous swellings, deep chasms, and sinuosities." "But," he continues, "what by far surpasses all admiration, and what in the first place moved me to present it to the attention of astronomers and philosophers, is this: namely, that we have discovered four planets, neither known nor observed by anyone before us, which have their periods around a certain big star previously known."[1] The "big star" was of course the planet Jupiter, and the "four planets" were the moons of Jupiter.

On October 4, 1923, Edwin Hubble focused the 100-inch reflector telescope at the Mount Wilson Observatory on one of the spiral arms of M31, known at that time as the Andromeda Nebula. The telescope was fitted with a camera that allowed long-term exposure of the photographic plate to the incoming light. Hubble took a forty-minute exposure and then on the following night repeated the procedure, increasing the exposure time by five minutes. When he examined the plates and compared them with earlier photographic examples, he determined that one of the objects photographed was a type of bright, pulsating star called a Cepheid. Such stars vary regularly in their brightness, becoming dimmer and brighter with periods from a few days to a few months; this first Cepheid that Hubble found in M31 had a period of 31.4 days,

---

1. Galileo Galilei, *Sidereus nuncius*, in vol. 5/3 of *Opere, Edizione Nationale* (Florence, 1892), 59ff.; cited in Alexandre Koyré, *From the Closed World to the Infinite Universe* (Baltimore: Johns Hopkins University Press, 1957), 89f.

and the curve formed by plotting the variation in its luminosity over this period was indisputably identifiable as that of a Cepheid. A decade earlier, Henrietta Leavitt had discovered that there is a strict correlation between the period of a Cepheid and its average luminosity; this discovery made it possible to determine a Cepheid's luminosity simply by measuring its period. This is precisely what Hubble did; having determined the average absolute luminosity, he had then only to measure directly the apparent luminosity in order then to calculate the distance to the star, using the inverse square law for light. Hubble's calculation showed that the Cepheid he had found in M31—and he soon found several more—was nearly a million light-years away, much too far for it to belong to the Milky Way.[2]

When things like these are seen—whether with unaided vision or with vision supplemented by instrumentation and calculation—once they are seen, it will never be quite the same again. With such discoveries a decisive, irreversible transition is made, even if decades may be required before the full implications can be worked out. When Tycho observed the new star, when Galileo turned his telescope to the moon and the stars, and when Hubble sighted a Cepheid in M31, our view of the cosmos was transformed once and for all. Once Tycho had observed a non-sublunary star that was not unchanging, as all non-sublunary bodies were supposed to be, the old Ptolemaic view was decisively undermined; it was only a matter of time—and in this case further discoveries—before it was completely dismantled. The enhanced observation of the moon's surface that Galileo achieved with his telescope offered confirming evidence by showing that this "first heaven" did not consist of an incorruptible substance different in kind from that of which the earth was composed. But if there was evident corruption in the lunar sphere and observable change even in stars beyond it, the suspicion could not but engulf the entire system of allegedly incorruptible spheres that the Ptolemaic theory supposed to fill the heaven.

Galileo's discovery of the moons of Jupiter was equally unsettling. For this discovery showed that not all bodies revolve around the earth, the centrality of which was thus put decisively into question. It would not be long before heliocentrism, already proposed by Copernicus, displaced the earth once and for all from the center of the cosmos.

2. See Hubble's account in Edwin Hubble, *The Realm of the Nebulae* (New Haven: Yale University Press, 1936), 83–101. Also Gale E. Christianson, *Edwin Hubble: Mariner of the Nebulae* (New York: Farrar, Straus and Giroux, 1995), 157f.

Galileo's third discovery was perhaps even more decisive: he found that through his telescope more than ten times more stars could be seen than by unaided vision. It was clear to him that this panoply of stars, invisible to the naked eye but visible to the extended vision granted by the telescope, must be more distant than those visible to unaided vision. But if there are stars at various distances from the earth, then they could not all be affixed to the great outermost sphere, which the Ptolemaic theory regarded as the absolute limit of the cosmos. In a letter to Ingoli, Galileo is explicit about the consequences of what he has seen: "You suppose that the stars of the firmament are, all of them, placed in the same orb: that is something the knowledge of which is so doubtful that it will never be proved." Then he adds that "no one in the world knows, nor can possibly know, not only what is the shape [of the firmament—that is, of the cosmos] but even whether it has any figure at all."[3]

When Hubble observed the Cepheid and with the aid of calculation determined that it lay far beyond the Milky Way, he showed thereby that M31, the so-called Andromeda Nebula, was not just a mass of dust and gas swirling near the edge of our galaxy, but rather another galaxy like the Milky Way itself, another "island universe," to use the phrase current at the time. By rendering visible and determinable the Andromeda Galaxy and then, shortly thereafter, still others like it, he showed that, contrary to what many astronomers right up to this time still maintained, the cosmos does not consist merely of the Milky Way surrounded by unlimited void but rather includes many other galaxies like our own. Subsequent observation with enhanced instrumentation has shown the number of galaxies to be enormous. Today it is estimated that there are as many as ten billion galaxies in the universe.[4]

Once such sights are seen, once instrumentation is sufficient to let them be seen and determined, a turn becomes imperative. Once we are no longer so earthbound as to require that the cosmos be centered here in our abode, our vision is opened to the beyond, to the enormous expanse of galaxies. Retreat is of course always possible, retreat to the familiar surroundings of our earth, this small planet orbiting one among a hundred billion suns in the Milky Way, itself one among billions of galaxies. It is of course possible to confine philosophical thought to what

---

3. Letter to Ingoli, in vol. 6 of *Opere, Edizione Nationale*, 525; cited in Koyré, *From the Closed World to the Infinite Universe*, 95f.

4. A much more detailed account of these discoveries and of their scientific and philosophical context is given in my *Logic of Imagination*, 247–57.

is manifest at this well-trodden locale, situated just off one of the spurs (the Orion Spur) of one of the spiral arms (the Perseus Arm) of the galaxy, some twenty-seven thousand light-years from the galactic center. And yet—need it be said?—such confinement cannot escape the charge of myopia and provincialism. Can it any longer be supposed as a matter of course that everything that in any way *is*, everything in this vast expanse, is manifest in the same manner as the things and events found on or near the surface of the earth? Is there not sufficient provocation to call into question such earthbound thinking? Has the time not come—now that sights once almost unthinkable have been seen—for thinking to turn to the beyond? Such a turn would not preclude interrogating our relatedness to the earth, perhaps in the manner initiated in Husserl's celebrated fragment from 1934 on the earth as *Ur-Arche*. But it would put an end to the confinement of thinking to the terrestrial surface.

This turn has sometimes been blocked, diverted, or at least rendered suspicious by reference to the alleged *a priori* character of modern scientific research. The supposition is that the findings of such research are always governed by theoretical structures projected in advance. Thus, philosophical thought would need to maintain critical distance from such findings, and instead of turning in directions indicated by these findings, it would take as its primary object of interrogation the projection allegedly sustaining them. And yet, whatever theoretical presuppositions may be operative, there are occasions when the findings break through those presuppositions, sometimes actually dictating against them, sometimes simply standing on their own and inviting interpretation in some measure independent of the *a priori* structure.

When Tycho Brahe saw a star suddenly appear, become extremely bright, and then in a few months fade away entirely, this finding—that stars can undergo such changes—was not rendered any less decisive by the fact that certain theoretical presuppositions were operative. To the extent that, in this case, those presuppositions were still entangled in the old Ptolemaic system, the finding dictated against them rather than being simply governed, even determined, by them. The finding was sufficiently decisive and independent that it was not simply reabsorbed into the *a priori* structure that had to some degree been operative. The fact that Galileo required the telescope in order to discover that there are moons orbiting Jupiter does not alter the situation in the least. Galileo's finding, that there are moons orbiting Jupiter, stood on its own quite apart from any theoretical project: there actually *are* moons orbiting Jupiter. Though Hubble's discovery required a much thicker layer of instrumentation and of established theoretical results, his finding—that there are other galaxies besides our own—emerged as a decisive result. There actually *are* other galaxies, and Hubble's finding opened the way not only to further observation-based investigation of them but also to more appropriate formulations of the theoretical questions prompted by such investigations.

On the occasion of such decisive breakthroughs, something is discovered that otherwise would remain concealed. Because they have not been seen before, because in some cases—as with moons orbiting another planet—nothing like them has ever been seen, these phenomena cannot but appear wondrous; they evoke wonder, and they prompt questions that run deeper than those addressed by empirically based research. Bound, above all, to wonder and questioning, philosophy cannot justify remaining aloof from these discoveries. To insist on maintaining critical distance from such findings to the extent of not engaging them philosophically amounts in the end to sheer evasion.

But how today are they to be engaged philosophically? How is philosophy to be activated in relation to such findings, granted the inversions and displacements that philosophy has, since Hegel, undergone? And what are some of the findings that can be especially provocative for thinking in our time?

A minimal yet sufficient schema is provided by the phenomenological concept of rigor, especially if it is borne in mind that this concept realizes in the form of an imperative a directive that goes back to Plato's appeal to τὸ πρᾶγμα αὐτό and that is sustained, if in varying degrees, in the history of philosophy, becoming finally explicit with Hegel. Philosophy would attend to phenomena in their self-showing. It would bind itself to manifestation, indeed so absolutely as to let what becomes manifest recoil upon itself. Thus, in attending to phenomena, it would be brought repeatedly back to itself, its very form of attending being adjusted and recast in view of the structures made manifest.

In carrying out the appeal to what shows itself to intuition—and this means, first of all, the founding mode, sense intuition—classical phenomenology had, almost from the start, to take into account aspects and structures that belong to objects of intuition but that are not themselves simply given to sense. Already, in drawing the distinction between natural things and natural elementals,[5] it has been observed that

---

5. See above, chap. 5.

phenomena, in their self-showing, include moments that do not simply show themselves. Specifically, it becomes evident that the directly sensed aspect (*Abschattung*) of an object bears reference to other aspects held in store; indeed, it implicates an entire horizon of other presently non-given aspects (an inner or lateral horizon). Although when an aspect is given intuitively, the others are not given, any one of them can, in principle, be given by altering one's perspective on the object. On the other hand, the horizon of all possible aspects, which is implicated by the presently intuited aspect, is something that *cannot be given* as such. One cannot see an object from everywhere at once, which would be tantamount to seeing it from nowhere. The lateral horizon cannot be deployed before us, cannot be spread out before our vision. It is a structure that, in this sense and to this extent, is invisible, an invisible structure that belongs to every visible thing and that determines its very visibility.

It is precisely with invisibility—with various modes of invisibility—that philosophy must deal in carrying out the cosmological turn. Invisibility is indeed already a factor in the transition broached by Galileo's findings. The roughness of the moon's surface, the satellites of Jupiter, the panoply of newly seen stars were all invisible, or nearly so, to natural, unaided vision. They became visible only to the enhanced vision made possible by the telescope. Even for this enhanced vision they retained a coefficient of invisibility: not only did they remain, even through the telescope, at a certain visual distance (unlike terrestrial objects, which can always be approached or brought near), but also, emphatically so at the time, they could be seen only from one perspective, that of the earth. The lateral horizon of such things remained purely virtual in a way that distinguished them from terrestrial things. Furthermore, as these and other unseen sights are brought into view, the sky, which is the limit for natural vision, gives way to the expanse of the cosmos. But to natural, unaided vision, the cosmos and the gigantic formations that come to be discovered—the galaxies, nebulae, clusters of galaxies, etc.—remain, even after their discovery, invisible as such. Even the Andromeda Galaxy, the only object beyond the Milky Way that is visible to the naked eye, appears merely as a point of light. Indeed, no matter how intensely one gazes out toward the galactic formations that one knows are there, all one sees is the radiant blue firmament or the star-studded nocturnal sky.

While such cosmic forms as galaxies, though invisible to natural vision, can be made visible by means of instrumentation, more recent observation-based research has come upon forms that are absolutely invisible. Such is very nearly the case with so-called dark matter.[6] It is entirely the case with black holes. Even to designate these as phenomena is to stretch the meaning of the term, if by phenomenon one normally means something that—at least under certain conditions such as the availability of a sufficiently powerful telescope—can show itself to vision, that is, can be made visible. For these forms do not under any conditions show themselves to sense.

If it could be called an object, one would have to say that a black hole is a very simple object. Yet as soon as one notes that it is centered in a singularity, it is evident that its structure in no way corresponds to that of a terrestrial thing (a thing having properties) or of a natural element such as wind or rain. A singularity is an intense concentration of very large mass (at least several times that of our sun) that converges asymptotically toward a point. Consequently, it has such enormous density that its gravity prevents even light from escaping; that is, the escape velocity is greater than the speed of light. There are various theories that have been put forth as to how black holes are formed; most agree that they result from the most extreme collapse of the core of a massive star that has exhausted its nuclear fuel. They are the remains—or the ghosts—of dead stars. Yet such theories are perhaps more constructive than observation-based.

As distance from a singularity increases, the escape velocity decreases, and at a certain distance it is equal to the speed of light. This distance, the so-called Schwarzschild radius, which measures approximately 3 km per solar mass, defines the extent of the black hole. The imaginary sphere described by this radius constitutes what is called the event horizon. It presents no features whatsoever, and amounts to the complete absence of a physical surface. The American physicist John Wheeler, who coined the term *black hole*, invented an apt metaphor when he said, "Black holes have no hair."[7] Especially in cases where a black hole is in rotation, it warps the space around it in an area extending

---

6. Dark matter, as well as other phenomena of this sort such as dark energy and cosmic microwave background radiation, is discussed in my *Logic of Imagination*, 264–67.

7. Since a black hole is revealed only by its external gravitational field, there are only two features that can be attributed to it: its mass and its angular momentum (see Mitchell Begelman and Martin Rees, *Gravity's Fatal Attraction: Black Holes in the Universe*, 2nd ed. [Cambridge: Cambridge University Press, 2010], 12). Yet these features must be distinguished entirely from properties, even quantitative properties, as classically determined, for they are in no way themselves manifest to sense.

beyond the event horizon called the ergosphere, an effect detectable by observation of the anomalous motion of bodies or masses of gas in the ergosphere.[8]

The event horizon is the place of no return for light. In its vicinity a shower of particles is produced, one of each pair escaping, the other falling into the black hole. It is the presence of this peculiarly configured array of particles that allows the event horizon, itself entirely invisible, to be detected.

Light—and everything else—that reaches the event horizon will disappear into the black hole. Since no light can escape it, it is entirely invisible—not really black at all, which would still be visible, but absolutely invisible. If a beam of light passes by a black hole at a certain theoretically determinable distance from the event horizon, it will execute a circular orbit around the black hole. This orbit defines what is called the photon sphere. If the light deviates from this sphere, it will spiral outward away from or inward toward the black hole. Popular writers like to portray astronauts who, orbiting in the photon sphere, would look straight ahead and see the backs of their heads.

Black holes are, then, entirely different in their basic structure from terrestrial things, from natural elements, and even from the more familiar cosmic forms such as stars and galaxies. Above all, they are, in their very structure, absolutely invisible in a way that no conceivable instrumentation could overcome. Indeed, they are accessible to observation-based research only indirectly, only because their presence, their enormous gravitational force, is indicated by other phenomena: either by huge masses of gas swirling around them, so-called accretion discs, or by stars orbiting them at anomalously high velocities. Supermassive black holes have by these methods been detected at the very center of many galaxies, including the Andromeda Galaxy and our own Milky Way. The mass of some such black holes borders on the inconceivable, indeed to such an extent that the descriptive terms transferred to them from ordinary terrestrial objects fall hopelessly short of saying what they intend: a giant galaxy, designated as M87, has a central black hole

---

8. A so-called Kerr black hole can behave like a spinning conductor in a magnetic field, thus producing a huge voltage difference (like a battery). In this way such black holes may be responsible for the jets in which matter traveling at nearly the speed of light extends for enormous distances. In such a case it could be said that something is actually extracted from the black hole, namely, the jet generated from its rotational energy (see ibid., 157–59).

with a mass estimated to be three billion times that of our sun; this black hole is itself larger than the entire solar system.

What is philosophically most provocative about black holes is their peculiar invisibility, a kind of invisibility hitherto unknown, indeed virtually inconceivable. It is not an invisibility that can be breached and converted in some degree into visibility. No telescope, no instrument of any sort, will allow us to see a black hole, for nothing, no electromagnetic radiation of any sort, escapes from it. Its resistance to vision is not comparable at all to that of a natural element, which, because we are encompassed by it, deprives us of the distance needed to get it in view. Neither is the invisibility of a black hole like that of the horizon of a perceptual object, which sequentially, though never as a whole, can be brought into view. Rather, the horizon of a black hole, its event horizon, displays no visibility whatsoever, displays nothing, almost as if it were nothing. And whereas a perceptual horizon serves to make an object genuinely visible as an object (rather than as a mere single aspect), an event horizon shelters the absolute invisibility of a black hole.

Ontologically considered, black holes represent a kind of being hitherto unknown, a kind of being entirely distinct from terrestrial things, natural elements, and even stars and galaxies. Black holes represent a kind of being that cannot be readily accommodated by the conceptual legacy of Western ontology. From what have been recognized as beings, they differ not just as one kind of thing differs from another, a natural thing, for instance, from one that is fabricated; the difference is, rather, one of basic ontological structure. It is a difference that interrupts the originary (and continuously renewed) Greek determination of being by reference to visibility. Being absolutely invisible, absolved from all visibility, black holes have no look whatsoever. Even if—to broach an extreme hypothetical—one were transported to the vicinity of a black hole so as to look upon it, there would be nothing to see other than a shower of flashing particles near the event horizon and perhaps, farther out, an accretion disc. No matter how directly or how closely one might look at it, the black hole itself would display no look at all. But if black holes have no look, they neither have an εἶδος nor assume the guise of an εἶδος. Their invisibility is thus also totally other than the invisibility of the intelligible. In their invisibility they are not set apart from the visible, as if separated by a χωρισμός. And yet, while belonging to the same domain as the visible, having even originated—if the genealogies are correct—from the collapse of highly visible stars (which may have exploded as supernovae, like the one that Tycho Brahe saw in 1572), black holes are almost entirely cut off from the visible. Their only concourse with the visible consists in dissolving the visibility of whatever approaches them and of repelling—or rather, infinitely withdrawing from—every effort to endow them with even a trace of visibility.

But then, if the ontological structure of black holes is determined by their absolute invisibility, by their utter absolution from all visibility, even from the invisible visibility of an εἶδος, then the bearing of philosophical thought cannot go unaffected. It would no longer suffice for the philosophical imperative to restrict thinking to what shows itself to intuition either sensible or eidetic, not even if the imperative were to accommodate a detour through λόγος, as in Socrates' second sailing. For a thinking so restricted could only remain mute, indeed void, in response to such monstrous hyperphenomena as black holes. There would now be required a new schema for thinking, a schema by which self-showing could proceed not only from the "itself" of what would show itself, that is, *von der Sache selbst*, but also by way of certain kinds of attestations yielding only traces, not the presence, of what would come to be itself shown.

The cosmological turn would require of philosophy that it take up critically and discerningly certain traces that can be provided only by observation-based research, supplemented by instrumentation and theoretical-mathematical elaborations. Yet, in its retracings, philosophy is bound to set in motion questions that run deeper than such research, interrogations that push toward the limit and that venture to resituate these expanded self-showings at the edge of whatever abyss opens up. And, above all, reenacting ever again its beginning, philosophy would hearken to the wonder evoked ever anew by things never before seen or even never to be seen in the starry heaven above, which is, at once, the inscrutable cosmos out there beyond.

7 COMING AS IF FROM NOWHERE

If there is any comprehensive imperative that has imposed itself on philosophy in recent times, it is that a new beginning be ventured. We hear this imperative especially as it was sounded more than a century ago when Nietzsche, in the voice of Zarathustra, called for a newly born thinking in the figure of the child: "The child is innocence and forgetting, a new beginning, play, a self-turning wheel, a first movement, a sacred yes-saying."[1] This call resounded in Heidegger's project of fundamental ontology, in which, purportedly for the first time, the question of the meaning of being would begin to be genuinely addressed. The call resounded even more distinctly when in the 1930s Heidegger ventured a thinking that sought to begin on the yonder side of an overcoming of metaphysics. The deconstructive strategies of Derrida, Nancy, and others take up this call and respond to the imperative.

Yet to begin with the imperative that a new beginning be ventured is, in a sense, to violate that imperative, for one will have begun not with the beginning demanded, but with the demand itself, with the imperative. In beginning anew, one will, then, already have responded to the imperative, and therefore any new beginning will be burdened with—not to say compromised by—a certain antecedence. Or to construe it otherwise: the imperative belongs to the very beginning that it demands.

Furthermore, the venturing of a new beginning is not itself anything new; it is not something only now undertaken, only now ventured. On the contrary, a new beginning has been repeatedly ventured in the history of metaphysics. Plato portrays Socrates as venturing

---

1. Friedrich Nietzsche, *Also Sprach Zarathustra*, in vol. VI/1 of *Werke*, 27.

a new beginning in what is called his second sailing, which is carried out through a decisive turn from φύσις to λόγος. Descartes ventures a new beginning by breaking with Scholasticism and extending universal doubt to its limit. Kant ventures a new beginning by submitting metaphysics to a critique that, in advance of metaphysics, would determine the possibilities and limits of reason. Hegel's venture of a new beginning takes the form of an absolute beginning, which in posing the question "With what must the science begin?" and indeed in the very undertaking of a phenomenology of spirit recognizes the complexity and reflexivity involved in beginning.

Thus, venturing a new beginning is not itself anything new; it is not itself a beginning, but rather a repetition of a decisive move that has repeatedly renewed and revitalized the most profound radicality of philosophy. On the other hand, to venture simply another beginning in distinction solely from a first beginning requires abstracting from the manifold resurgence of the radical motif and positing a substantial unity underlying the entire history of metaphysics, from which, then, the other beginning can be set apart. Whether the history of metaphysics displays any such uniformity is—to say the least—highly questionable. In order to mark this questionableness and so to keep the assumption of such uniformity at a distance, it needs to be stressed that the word *metaphysics* is suspended between singular and plural.

Because of its antecedent imperative, and especially because it is a repetition of a move manifestly undertaken in the history of philosophy, the venture of a new beginning is necessarily referred back to that history. There is no beginning simply anew, as with a *tabula rasa*, but rather a beginning is always already situated in a history. In order to be true to the radical motif of philosophy, it is necessary that the venture—or adventure—of a new beginning take cognizance of this situatedness. The imperative is, then, not only to venture a new beginning, but to do so in a way that goes back into the history of metaphysics. It may well be in this retreat that certain resources, certain possibilities, for a new beginning can be uncovered.

The complexity involved in venturing a new beginning recurs in more specific form in the effort to rethink the sense of imagination within the new beginning portended for our time in Nietzsche's image of the child. How, in this new beginning, is imagination to be thought? This question cannot simply be addressed directly and straightforwardly, for in the very formulation there is a tension that forces the question to recoil on itself and thus to pose a question of the question, to the question. The tension is between, on the one side, the prospect of a new beginning that, like the child, would be innocence and forgetting and, on the other side, the compound of presupposed language and conceptuality that is put in force as soon as one takes up any theme that, as with imagination, has from the outset been developed in relation to the parameters of metaphysical thinking. In posing the question of imagination, all the connections that this conception sustains are also drawn into the sphere of the new beginning, contaminating its state of innocence and limiting its forgetting. In the form of imagination the child will not, it seems, be newly born at all, but only reborn in a guise that cannot but retain certain features from its previous incarnations.

And yet, there is something that prevents this tension from abruptly immobilizing the question, a certain factor that eases it and opens a space for the question. It is the fact that in the history of metaphysics, imagination is not simply appropriated. Again and again, from Plato on, metaphysics is compelled to set imagination at a distance, to establish a refuge (such as pure practical reason or the final haven of dialectic), a refuge that would be free from the play of imagination, a play often innocent of—even oblivious to—the difference between truth and semblance, a play that, from beyond good and evil, never ceases to celebrate—to say yes to—the sensuous. Nothing is more telling in this regard than the judgment pronounced by Pico della Mirandola in his treatise *On the Imagination*. Having granted that the soul, in its embodiment, must rely on imagination to supply it with images, Pico then charges imagination with producing "all monstrous opinions and the defects of all judgments." He condemns imagination, calling it "vain and wandering," and confesses that it is in order to demonstrate this that he has written his treatise.[2] Thus, if metaphysics would aim at the true and the good, it must protect itself from imagination, must keep this not so innocent play at a safe distance. At best, imagination will only have been the errant stepchild of metaphysics.

To take up again the question of imagination, but now within a new beginning attuned to the Nietzschean imperative, has therefore a certain appropriateness, for this conception, even though taken over, has a certain intrinsic resistance to metaphysics—or at least to certain

---

2. Gianfrancesco Pico della Mirandola, *On the Imagination*, Latin text with English translation by Harry Caplan, in vol. 16 of *Cornell Studies in English* (New Haven: Yale University Press, 1930), 29. See my discussion in *Delimitations*, chap. 1.

dominant strains within the history of metaphysics. Having been kept at a distance from the heartland of metaphysics, it has a capacity now to aid in setting metaphysics—or at least certain principal motifs of metaphysics—at a distance. In this respect, rethinking imagination can contribute—perhaps uniquely—to the venture of a new beginning, in which, though indeed drawn back into the history of metaphysics, thinking would put metaphysics, in its multiple occurrences, more radically in question, thereby exposing hitherto unheeded openings.

There are, no doubt, several avenues by which, in thinking imagination anew and in order to think it anew, one can turn back into the history of metaphysics in a way that furthers such thinking by exposing certain junctures from which such thinking might set out. The avenue to be followed here is one that runs through two distinct yet parallel mutations. Both mutations are broached—or at least their points of departure are established—in the history of metaphysics. These starting points are, in fact, fissures or breaches in what might seem the uniform landscape of metaphysics, tears, as it were, in its fabric. As such, they open the way toward thinking imagination anew. One such point occurs at the outset of metaphysics, at certain junctures in the Platonic dialogues where the metaphysical parameters have not yet been so thoroughly stabilized. The other is generated by certain consequences of the Kantian critical project and comes to the surface in Fichte's reconfiguration of that project.

We have observed that Pico, in characterizing imagination, identifies two opposed tendencies, one that is veracious and salutary, another that is errant and mendacious. The ascription of such a twofold character to imagination does not, however, originate with Pico; neither is he the last to posit such a differentiation. On the contrary, the distinction runs throughout much of the history of metaphysics, forming a complex strand of that history as various representations and designations of the respective sides gain prominence. The differentiation between the two sides or forms is borne by the distinction between the two Latin designations *imaginatio* and *phantasia*, though the precise sense of the distinction and the specific character of each form vary enormously in the course of this history.[3]

The distinction derives from the difference between the two forms designated in Plato's *Republic* by the terms εἰκασία and φαντασία. In this context these are not yet conjoined as two forms of the same power,

---

3. See my account of this history in *Force of Imagination*, chap. 2.

nor even as powers that are somehow akin; their association and hence the distinction as such are established only later in Proclus' commentary on the *Republic*. It is especially in the Platonic treatment of the first of these forms, εἰκασία, that one can discern the starting point that, largely suppressed in the history of metaphysics, sets in motion one of the mutations that imagination undergoes in the present venture of a new beginning.

The term εἰκασία occurs in the Socratic account of the divided line, which represents the course by which philosophy would make its ascent toward true being and the final good; it is the way on which the soul is turned around and engaged in παιδεία. Derived from the word εἰκών, translatable as *image* or *semblance*, εἰκασία is characterized as the capacity to apprehend images. More precisely, as elaborated through the corresponding image of the cave, εἰκασία is the capacity to apprehend, in and through an image, the original of which it is an image or semblance—the capacity, for instance, to recognize in a picture of Polemarchus the man Polemarchus himself. Though εἰκασία is explicitly assigned only to the lowest of the segments of the divided line—assuming the usual vertical representation—the further elaboration indicates that much the same capacity is also operative at other levels, so that the term may, with some justification, be extended to nearly the entire course that philosophy would traverse. In the movement up the line, there would occur reiterated passage of vision through an image to the original of which it is an image; such passage from image to original is precisely what would drive the philosophical ascent. The capacity required for this passage would consist in the ability to catch a glimpse of the original in the image so as then to extend one's vision onward to apprehend the original itself. Thus, εἰκασία would enable vision to move repeatedly through image to original, each original then serving, in turn, as an image from which vision would again move on to its original. Yet, in this movement there is not only the passage onward to the original but also another constituent move, namely, the recognition that the image is an image and not simply an original. Thus, from the moment one's vision advances from image to original, it also circles back to the image, recognizing its character as an image. Thus, εἰκασία involves a double operation, that is, two operations with opposite directionalities that are, on the other hand, bound together. It belongs to εἰκασία not only to release these operations, but also to hold them together so that precisely in recognizing the image as an image one advances toward the original, and conversely.

Two distinctive features of εἰκασία thus come to light. The first lies in the fact that its relation to images is not a simple, direct relation; rather, it is a double relation, a holding together of two operations with opposite directionalities, setting the original forth from the image while also marking the image as an image. The second feature lies in the fact that εἰκασία is not a relatedness to mere images in contrast to the things that truly are. Rather, the images that εἰκασία engages are precisely images that have the character of imaging—even if from a distance—the things that truly are; and εἰκασία is thus a power, not merely for entertaining mere images, but for advancing toward being.

These two features thoroughly distinguish εἰκασία from imagination as it is conceived in recent reductive accounts, which regard it merely as a power of entertaining freely formed images. These reductive accounts—Sartre's and Casey's, for example—exemplify the way in which concepts rigorously forged in the history of philosophy can come to be exhausted and can collapse into near-trivialities. But in the case of imagination there was always resistance that kept it somewhat apart from metaphysics and from certain corrosive forces attached to metaphysics, even though—as these examples show—it was never entirely immune. Features such as these two, held in reserve, can provide an opening for thinking imagination anew.

The second of the two forms described in the *Republic* is φαντασία, which is subsequently compounded with εἰκασία into what will come to be translated as *imagination*. As described by Socrates, φαντασία is mimetic in character: it is the capacity to produce an image or semblance of things, an image that resembles what it images but that, because it is only a resemblance and not the thing itself, can deceive, keeping its beholders at a distance from the thing itself. Because of this power of deception, φαντασία is submitted to criticism and in the best city would be subject to censorship. Both as the evocation of the image through words—that is, as poetry—and as actual representation in painting, φαντασία is capable of deceiving and corrupting those who are exposed to its productions, keeping them at a remove from the truth. It is this Socratic description that is resounded in Pico's condemnation of imagination nearly two millennia later.

But suppose now, in order to clear the space of a new beginning, one moves outside this critical perspective and considers phantasy as it operates either purely or in relation to words, setting aside the more complex case of the phantastics of painting. This operation readily proves to be more complex than might have been supposed.

Suppose one imagines a dragon of the awesome Chinese sort, doing so with or without the word *lóng*, which designates such a creature, with or without observing how in the Chinese characters (龙, 龍) one can discern a shape suggestive of such a creature,[4] with or without explicitly recalling pictures one has seen of Chinese dragons. Since such creatures, which the ancient Chinese regarded as the force of life itself, tend—so it is said—to appear suddenly only to disappear again, they display a special affinity to phantasy, beyond their being, as we say, mere figments of imagination.

In any case, suppose one imagines—that is, evokes in phantasy—such a creature soaring through the clouds, its claws extended, its scales glistening. In order for one to imagine seeing the dragon, the look of the creature must come before one's inner vision, must be present to one's phantasy, present to—as we say—the mind's eye. Yet, as merely imagined, the dragon is not perceptually given; there are, one assumes, no dragons actually existing such that one could see them as one sees birds, trees, and mountains. In the case of the dragon, its look must be brought forth by the activity of imagining, that is, specifically, by phantasizing. In order that the look of the dragon be intuitively given, in order that it be present to the inner vision, this givenness must be produced precisely in and through the imagining. In such a case, imagination—in the mode of phantasy—*gives to itself* that which is imagined, brings it forth in such a way that it, in turn, is given to the inner vision that belongs to imagining. Furthermore, once the look of the dragon has been brought forth, it must be sustained if it is to remain present to one's inner vision and not, as dragons are wont to do, abruptly disappear. Yet there is nothing to sustain it other than the self-giving, and so it must be continually brought forth through such autodonation. The dragon must be held there in phantasy, must be continually brought forth precisely as it is intuited. The production of the image belongs no less to the structure of phantasy than does the vision of it in the mind's eye. Thus, phantasy, too, proves to involve a double operation: in and through the imagining, the phantasy image is both brought forth and intuited. Hence, the operation of phantastic imagination must be such as to carry out, but also to hold together, the productive and the intuitive moments in their opposite directionalities. Phantastic imagination must circulate between

---

4. See the account in David Hinton, *Hunger Mountain* (Boston: Shambhala, 2012), 74–79.

these two opposed operations so as, through this circulation, through this hovering between them, to hold them together.

Both the recovery of εἰκασία and the analysis of phantasy serve to bring to light the character of imagination as holding together in their opposition two moments that are opposed in their governing directionality. It is through the emergence of this character that the first of the two mutations of imagination is broached, the mutations through which imagination assumes the form in which it is to be redetermined within the venture of a new beginning. It is only in the final phase of the history of metaphysics that this character begins to be explicitly grasped, namely, in German Idealism. In this context there is no more succinct formulation than that given in Schelling's *System of Transcendental Idealism*: "That alone through which we are capable of thinking, and of holding together, what is contradictory [is] imagination."[5] The distinctive operation in which it displays this character is designated by the word *Schweben*—let us say: hovering. The sense of the word is that imagination suspends itself between the opposed moments, wavering between them rather than settling on one or the other, while circulating or oscillating between them so as to bond them together as a dyad of moments that retain nonetheless their mutual opposition.

Yet it belongs equally to this mutation that through such an operation, imagination launches an advance to being. Such is most explicit in the case of εἰκασία, for the progression from image to original is precisely an advance to being. In the case of phantasy, this connection becomes evident only if the disclosive capacity of phantastic images is taken into account. Whether evoked through words, as in poetry and literature generally, or actually produced, as in painting, images display a capacity to reveal the things they image, to open onto their truth, even if, as the Socratic account emphasizes in its specifically political context, they also have the power to conceal. To the Chinese sensibility the image of the dragon is not something totally disconnected from life but reveals something of its profound animation. In the celebrated dictum by Paul Klee: "Art does not reproduce the visible but makes visible."[6]

Within the context of German Idealism, the advance to being that is enabled by imagination is understood not just as gaining insight into a predetermined, preconstituted realm of being, but rather as the advance in and through which being is first brought forth as such, as the

---

5. F. W. J. Schelling, *System des transzendentalen Idealismus*, 295–96.
6. Paul Klee, "Schöpferische Konfession," in *Kunst-Lehre* (Leipzig: Reclam, 1987), 60.

operation by which things first become manifest to the advance of insight. In the words of Fichte's *Wissenschaftslehre*: "It is therefore here taught that all reality—*for us* being understood, as it cannot be otherwise understood in a system of transcendental philosophy—is brought forth solely by the imagination."[7]

As it emerges through its mutation, imagination assumes the form of a power that, through its hovering between opposed moments so as to hold them together in their opposition, is effective in letting things come forth into their manifestness. It is preeminently through imagination that things as such and even the unseen truths about them come to light for us.

The second of the mutations through which the form of imagination passes as it emerges in the venture of the present new beginning is distinct from the first, though the two are linked and at a certain point intersect in such a way that this other mutation interrupts the first. The point of departure of the second mutation is also to be found at certain junctures—or breaches—in the history of metaphysics. It is foreshadowed in the indecision (demonstrated in recent studies)[8] that Aristotle displays as to whether φαντασία is a power of the soul and in the corresponding indecision in Kant as to whether imagination is to be classified as a power (*Vermögen*) of the subject. In such indecision there is perhaps a trace of the broad tendency of metaphysics to keep imagination safely at bay. The relevant point of departure is foreshadowed also in Neoplatonism, specifically in Iamblichus, who subordinates human φαντασία to the gift of divine epiphanies. According to Iamblichus, what draws the human soul into the advance to being is nothing in the soul itself but rather the gift of light, the more-than-human φαντασία that comes upon us, to which, in turn, mere human φαντασία is bound to submit and respond.[9]

Yet the starting point of the second mutation comes fully to light in the radical consequence that Fichte draws from the Kantian critical project. In the *Critique of Pure Reason*, imagination is already engaged as the power that yokes together sense and intelligence, intuition and

---

7. J. G. Fichte, *Grundlage der gesammten Wissenscaftslehre*, in vol. 1 of *Werke*, 227.
8. The reference is to the studies by Eva Brann (on Aristotle) and Rodolphe Gasché (on Kant) discussed in my *Force of Imagination*, 44–45, 70.
9. Iamblichus' conception of φαντασία and his distinction between human φαντασία and more-than-human φαντασία or divine epiphanies is expounded in his work *On the Mysteries*. A detailed account is given in my *Force of Imagination*, 60–63, 74.

thought, in such a way that experience of objects and indeed objects themselves become possible. The consequence that Fichte draws is that it is only in relation to an object that there can be a subject, that is, that the very constitution of a subject requires the bringing-forth of objects that is accomplished solely—or at least preeminently—by imagination. Thus, Fichte concludes that imagination is the ground of the possibility of the subject. But in this case imagination can no longer be conceived as a power *of* the subject, since it is presupposed by the very constitution of the subject. A reversal is thus broached: rather than imagination belonging as a power to subjectivity, subjectivity will stem from the operation of imagination.

Therefore, the mutation to which imagination comes to be submitted results from its liberation from the subject. No longer determined as a power (δύναμις, *Vermögen*) of the soul or of the subject, it can be twisted free of any such belonging. It is no longer to be conceived as something possessed by a psychic entity or substance, as a capacity at the disposal of such an agent, as a power to be actualized by the psyche. Even the hovering attributed to it through the first mutation is to be freed of the subject; it is no longer to be determined as an activity of a subject made possible through a power possessed by the subject. This liberation from the subject marks the point where this other mutation intersects with and interrupts the first mutation. There remains, then, only the hovering without anything that hovers, without anything underlying (ὑποκείμενον). It is not unlike the flashing of lightning. Though our grammar requires us to say that lightning flashes, there is, in fact, no thing, the lightning, behind the flashing, no agent that flashes; rather, the lightning is nothing other than the flashing. So it is also with the hovering of imagination. There is only the hovering in the wake of which things may then come to light, may become manifest to humans.

The consequences of this development are virtually unlimited in their deconstructive effect on the classical concepts that have shaped the basic conception of the human throughout much of the history of metaphysics. If the manifestation of things to humans is subordinate to the hovering imagination, that is, if imagination, releasing things into the light, is not grounded in something within the human that is underlying, then the very determination of the human as essentially soul or subject is effaced. The space of another determination of the human is thus opened. Such a determination would no longer proceed from the classical concepts of οὐσία and ψυχή, nor from all that comes in the train of these ancient determinations, such concepts as *substantia*, *res cogitans*, etc.; rather, it would set out from the configuration of the moments that belong to the self-showing of things. Thus would a new conception of the human be broached within the project of such a new beginning as is presently being ventured.

If the hovering of imagination is not activated through the power of a subject, if it is not grounded in something underlying within the human, then its occurrence is most aptly described by saying that it simply arrives, that it comes without any ground or origin becoming manifest, that it comes as if from nowhere. This *nowhere* has often been given a name, especially in relation to poetic imagination; the Greeks often named it mythically, calling it Apollo. Such mythical naming is not to be simply dismissed, for it is a preeminent way in which imagination, drawing on such natural elements as light and fire, engages the human in reflective discourse and representation.

Yet, granted that imagination comes as if from nowhere, it cannot, nonetheless, eventuate as something utterly beyond the human. Coming as if from nowhere, the hovering of imagination lets things come to light for humans; it has the character of a pure luminous gift, of a gift without any manifest origin. As with every gift, there comes with it the entreaty that we receive it with gratitude, though in the instance of imagination the gratitude called for is directed at no one, at no source of the gift. Receiving the gift with gratitude, welcoming it, cannot, however, occur as a deliberate act, not, at least, at the level at which imagination first lets things come to light. For any deliberate act already presupposes a context in which things are manifest; prior to any such act, the configuration of manifestation must already have taken shape; yet this draft is possible only if imagination has already come upon the scene, indeed even before it actually becomes a scene. Humans will, then, always already be bound to the imperative to welcome the coming—as if from nowhere—of imagination. This imperative will also harbor the requirement that the gift always be relinquished rather than possessed, that is, rather than a claim being staked to possess it, as if it were—or could become—a power of a subject. The *always already* that characterizes the human reception of imagination as it comes as if from nowhere is thus unassimilable to the classical concept of the *a priori*. As with the imperative that a new beginning be ventured (the imperative with which we began), the antecedence that releases the imperative of imagination is decisive. And the human bond to this imperative can, if thought through in its articulation, perhaps provide a locus from which the ἦθος of the human can, in the new beginning, be thought.

In any case, in venturing to think imagination anew, one will take it as coming as if from nowhere to hover over the luminous presence of things, as the Greeks dreamed of Apollo coming unaccountably to guide the hand of the poet.

8 THE PLURALITY OF NATURE AND THE DISINTEGRATION OF DIFFERENCE

One ought to begin at the beginning. This, at any rate, is what Timaeus prescribes, even though not quite at the beginning of the dialogue that bears his name. Moreover, this dialogue itself, as it proceeds, proves—quite remarkably—not to have begun at the beginning. Indeed, it becomes evident in the course of the dialogue that it has so utterly violated Timaeus' prescription that it becomes imperative for it to begin again, not just once, but twice, its beginnings thus matching the counting, the 1, 2, 3, with which it in fact begins.

All of Timaeus' discourses, including those in which finally he returns to a new beginning, concern nature. In the first of his three discourses, he describes the way in which the god constructs the cosmos by proceeding in much the same manner as would an artisan fabricating a product, that is, in the manner prescribed by the paradigm of ποίησις. Yet, a return to the beginning becomes imperative once the constraint of necessity imposes itself; the new beginning thus launched leads to discourse on a kind of nature before nature, namely, the χώρα and, within it, the traces of the elements. Then comes the second return, which opens the final discourse describing the way in which nature in a more proper sense—from the simple elements up to the most complex creatures—is finally brought about. Thus, beginning with nature, the returns to the beginning prove to be returns to nature in another guise.

The necessity of these returns attests that beginnings are rarely—perhaps never—simple. Even when Timaeus says, "With regard to everything it is most important [μέγιστον] to begin at the natural beginning,"[1] it is possible to hear him, in the word μέγιστον, also hint-

---

1. Plato, *Timaeus* 29b.

THE PLURALITY OF NATURE 105

ing that to begin at what is by nature the beginning (κατὰ φύσιν ἀρχή) may also be most excessive. Nonetheless, whatever suspicions may have been aroused—above all, the suspicion that a return to the beginning may become imperative—one must in some manner begin; and it seems that one cannot do better than to begin—or at least seek to begin—at the beginning.

To do so is, in the present instance, already to engage in a return to the beginning, even if in another sense. For to take up the themes of plurality and difference requires engagement with the history of metaphysics in which these concepts have been forged. In turn, this requires an interrogation of the alleged end or exhaustion of metaphysics and its bearing on these concepts. Yet, such an interrogation can be carried out only by engaging also in a return to the beginning of metaphysics.

Metaphysics—or rather, what only later, retrospectively, came to be called metaphysics—is said to begin with Plato—even though there are most certainly other, quite different strands in the Platonic texts, and even though the proper name remains problematic, since Plato never speaks in the dialogues designated by his name. Yet, granted that a beginning highly pertinent to—if not *of*—metaphysics is woven into the Platonic dialogues, it is most conspicuous in the texts in which being is thought as one, in distinction from the many, which are composed of a mixture of being and non-being and so never fully are themselves. Correlatively, being as one is thought as νοητόν, as accessible only to νοῦς, as intelligible, in distinction from the many conceived as αἰσθητά, as presented to sense, as sensible and thus as things of nature. The kinds of λόγος are also distinguished along the same line: since what is said in λόγος corresponds precisely to the νοητά, a coherent λόγος directed at the sensible, an εἰκὼς λόγος, is possible only to the extent that the νοητά, the intelligible ones, are manifest in the sensible many. More precisely, the very possibility of discourse, spoken or silent, depends on the determining presence of the intelligible in the sensible. In every case a one must govern the many, installing the determinacy by which each of the many is what it is, the determinacy that, in turn, can be expressed in λόγος.

The thinking of being as one over against the sensible many that go to make up nature is initiated in an exemplary way in the *Theaetetus*, the very dialogue in which Socrates identifies the beginning of philosophy. This identification occurs when, in response to a series of aporias—of "wonderful and laughable things," as they are called—Theaetetus says performatively, "I wonder excessively [ὑπερφυῶς ... θαυμάζω]." Socrates then responds, in turn, by identifying wonder as the beginning of philosophy.[2] It is not coincidental that this identification occurs within an extended discussion of the relation between knowing and sense, a discussion that culminates in a passage in which Socrates traces a decisive exceeding of sense. Referring to the multiplicity of perceptions, most notably those given through different senses, Socrates describes the movement by which they are "stretched together toward some one look."[3] This one look (ἰδέα) he characterizes by the word κοινόν, the common, that which multiple perceptions have in common. Among the κοινά that he mentions are included the "is" and the "is not," as well as the same (τὸ ταυτόν) and the other (τὸ ἕτερον). Unlike the manifold perceptions, the κοινά are not to be apprehended by sense but only insofar as "the soul by itself stretches itself toward them."[4] Just as the κοινά, each of which is itself one, exceed in each case the manifold of perceptions, so, in apprehending them, the soul stretches itself beyond the reach of sense, exceeding all that is offered to sense. While beginning, as Socrates says, *in* wonder, philosophy begins *with* this self-stretching from the many to the one by which they are gathered and determined—that is, by stretching itself from nature to that which exceeds nature, by stretching itself beyond nature. It is through this move that a way is provided beyond the indeterminacy and muteness that, as the *Theaetetus* demonstrates, are the inevitable results of confinement to mere sense.

This move from the manifold of sense to the unitary κοινά is regarded as the founding distinction of what comes to be called metaphysics. In its elaboration each κοινόν is determined as being what it is, as being absolutely itself, in no way other than itself, entirely the same as itself, utterly selfsame in its pure determinacy.

Among the consequences of this originary determination—which is also the determination of the originary, of ἀρχή—there are two that need especially to be noted. The first is that the κοινά are devoid of movement, are unchanging, since the effect of change would be to render the κοινόν other than itself, thus violating its very determination as such. It is highly significant that this character is derivative: it is not because they are unchanging that the κοινά are selfsame; rather, because they are determined as selfsame, they must be devoid of movement—or,

---

2. Plato, *Theaetetus* 155c. See my extended discussion in *The Figure of Nature*, chap. 5.
3. Plato, *Theaetetus* 184d.
4. Ibid. 186a.

more precisely, of any movement that would violate their selfsameness. The second consequence is that each κοινόν is a discrete one that cannot undergo mixing or blending with others. As discrete ones, the κοινά are countable, can be numbered, even if no counting can exhaust their number. They are arithmetic in character.

But now—so it appears—all this is at an end. The story that has been told now for more than a century is that metaphysics has run its course. Running through all possible configurations of intelligible ones over against the manifold of sense, metaphysics comes finally to the point where, with Hegel, selfsame, determining oneness is thought as the *Aufhebung* of otherness through which spirit returns to itself, carrying out its odyssey of self-presence. Beyond these configurations there remains only the possibility of complete inversion, first broached by Marx and then, with Nietzsche, realized to such an extent that the very schema of intelligible/sensible is exposed to displacement. Thus, in running its course, driven on—so it would appear—by some still to be disclosed necessity, metaphysics would have exhausted its possibilities, and that exhaustion would be attested finally by the inversion of its founding distinction.

With the inversion and displacement—that is, once the "true world" has finally become a fable—the task that imposes itself is to think being otherwise than as selfsame, noetic one, to think it also otherwise than as the various reconfigurations assumed in the history of metaphysics, for instance, that of the self-identical transcendental subject constitutive of the being of objects. It is not, however, a matter of simply abandoning the noetic moment; rather, what is required is that its status as ἀρχή be compromised by exposing an operation both anterior to it and decisive for it. What is required is a thinking that exceeds being in its metaphysical determination, a thinking in excess of being. But, in turn, once the archaic status of the noetic one is compromised, the sensible manifold will have been released from its rigorous governance. The many will, in varying degrees, have escaped the yoke of the one, and nature will have been freed. What within metaphysics took the form of mere multiplicity now becomes free plurality. Nature as plurality is returned to itself.

Since the story was told and indeed completed in the very telling, efforts to think beyond being have been ventured along various paths. Here it must suffice to outline only two such ways and to offer with respect to each only minimal indications. The first is the way charted by Heidegger's project. Its direction is set from the beginning, displayed in

Heidegger's very proposal to take up the question, not simply of being, but of the meaning or sense of being (*der Sinn von Sein*). For what is thereby proposed is to think beyond being to the horizon from which being is determined as such. Initially Heidegger identifies this beyond as the transcendental horizon of time, preliminarily as the *Zeitlichkeit des Daseins* and, in what would have been the completion of the project, as the *Temporalität des Seins*. Yet the project, hyperontological from the outset, is interrupted; or rather, deferring completion, it mutates in ways that render it ever more distinctively a thinking beyond being. Orientation to the meaning of being gives way to discourse on the truth of being, on the unconcealment that lets things come to presence as being what they are. The complex of unconcealment/concealment, of openness and mystery—that is ἀλήθεια—is, in turn, interrogated along several different paths, which are marked by such words as *Ereignis, Geschick des Seins, Gestell,* and *Kehre*.

Perhaps the most direct of these paths is that traced, with rare lucidity, in the late essay "The End of Philosophy and the Task of Thinking." Taking as his point of departure the phenomenological appeal to the things themselves (*zu den Sachen selbst*), Heidegger poses the question: What remains unthought in this appeal? In effect, the question asks: What is required in order for things to show themselves, in order for them to shine forth in their presence? In response, he writes: "Such shining necessarily occurs in a brightness [*in einer Helle*]. Only through brightness can what shines show itself, i.e., shine. But brightness in its turn occurs only within an open and free region [*in einem Offenen, Freien*], which it may illuminate here and there, now and then. Brightness plays in the open region and contends there with darkness."[5] The move here regresses—or rather, progresses—to the previously unthought condition. Something can come to be present, can show itself, only by shining forth. Yet, shining requires brightness; only where there is brightness, only in the light, can something shine so as to show itself. But—and this is the decisive step—brightness can occur only within a certain space, only, so to speak, out in the open where there is space for the free play of light. Heidegger concludes: "We call this openness, which grants a possible letting-shine and a showing, the clearing [*die Lichtung*]."[6] He declares that it is the clearing that remains unthought in the appeal to the things themselves, and indeed in the entire history of

---

5. Martin Heidegger, *Zur Sache des Denkens* (Tübingen: Max Niemeyer, 1969), 71.
6. Ibid.

THE PLURALITY OF NATURE   109

philosophy (as metaphysics). He intensifies his declaration by repeating the move leading to the clearing, but now with explicit reference to the beginning of philosophy, that is, to Plato. He refers to the Platonic words for being, namely, ἰδέα and εἶδος, and translates them as *Aussehen*—in English: *look*, in the sense of the look that something shows when one looks at it. Heidegger continues: "Look, however, is a manner of presence." His point is that it is by way of its look, by the shining forth of its look, that something can come to be present as what it is. Then—decisively—he concludes: "No look without light—Plato already knew this. But there is no light and no brightness without the clearing."[7]

While this move to the beyond of being may appear to leave nature and the things of nature behind, it can hardly go unnoticed how thoroughly the language relies on and indeed is animated by words descriptive of natural phenomena. For it is precisely upon the expanse of nature that sunlight is cast, and it is within a forest that a clearing can occur. These expressions cannot simply be set aside as mere metaphors. Of what could light be a metaphor except—as since Plato—of a kind of illumination that would belong necessarily to the domain of the now vanquished νοητά? Furthermore, according to Heidegger's own analysis, metaphoricity presupposes the very distinctions that are here being put in question.

Nature cannot, then, be abandoned in order to take one's stand beyond, indeed in a beyond that is beyond being and thus still farther beyond all that has to do with nature. As long as this bond to nature remains unacknowledged and is not deliberately brought into the discourse, that discourse will—as Heidegger often does—tend toward abstractness and aridity. This is indeed a proclivity that can be discerned already in *Being and Time* despite its concreteness in many other respects.[8]

According to Heidegger, then, it is the clearing that is now to be thought, to be thought beyond being and its illumination. Yet, the clearing can be rigorously thought as in excess of being only if this thinking also blocks the errancy that would draw the beyond back toward reappropriation to being. Thinking beyond being must remain continually on guard against falling back into the mere ontic-ontological circuit. Heidegger does not hesitate to employ orthographic means to mark the

---

7. Ibid., 74.
8. See my discussion under the title "Twisting Free—Being to an Extent Sensible," chap. 3 of *Echoes: After Heidegger* (Bloomington: Indiana University Press, 1990), 76–96.

mutation of being that would serve to break any such fall: on occasion he crosses out the word *being*, and even more persistently he alters its spelling, adopting the old form *Seyn*.

And yet, in compromising being and marking its demise as ἀρχή, such thinking beyond being cannot but have a bearing on the remains of the ontic-ontological circuit; it cannot but have the effect of freeing the things of nature from the yoke of being. In *Contributions to Philosophy* Heidegger touches repeatedly on this effect, observing that the task is "to restore beings from out of the truth of beyng." He refers to such restoration as to be accomplished insofar as, for instance, beings come to presence "in the open of the strife between earth and world."[9] Thus, while resolutely directed to the beyond of being, such thinking would also open—would let be opened—a free space of things, a space of open plurality, of the plurality of nature.

A second way of thinking beyond being is ventured in the work of Derrida, and nowhere more insistently than in the lecture text entitled "La Différance." By its own testimony this text is a sheaf (*un faisceau*), a weaving together of different strands—a weaving, however, rather more like that of Penelope than like that of the texts of metaphysics. Its would-be beginning already unravels itself. It reads: "I will speak, therefore, of a letter."[10] The word "therefore" (*donc*) effects the unraveling, for it is a word that belongs properly to a conclusion following a chain of premises, not at a beginning. One can properly say "therefore" only if something else precedes this saying; that is, the word here gestures toward something preceding, and therefore in the words with which the text would begin there is a disclaimer, an erasure, an unweaving, of its status as beginning. Not long after this beginning that is yet no beginning, Derrida writes: "I will not know where to begin to trace the sheaf";[11] for, as he explains, it is a matter of putting in question the value of ἀρχή. With this move the text will already have set its sights beyond being, and in another sense will already have begun.

The letter of which Derrida will, therefore, speak is the first in the alphabet, the leading character, as it were, in what is alleged to be phonetic writing. He speaks of the orthographic strategy by which the substitution of the letter *a* extends the senses of the noun corresponding

---

9. Heidegger, *Beiträge zur Philosophie*, vol. 65 of *Gesamtausgabe* (Frankfurt a.M.: Vittorio Klostermann, 1989), §4.
10. Jacques Derrida, *Marges de la Philosophie* (Paris: Les Éditions de Minuit, 1972), 3.
11. Ibid., 6.

to the verb *différer* to the point where its extension matches that of the verb; in addition, the suffix *-ance* (referring to the present participle) serves to suspend the word *différance* undecidedly between active and passive voice, rendering it more like the middle voice.

What, then, is at stake in this fabricated word, which is thereby—and for other reasons, too—not a word? Derrida says: "It is the determination of being as presence or as beingness that is therefore interrogated by the thought of *différance*."[12] Aside from the non-word *différance*, the statement directly translates the Heideggerian idiom of *Seiendheit*, which designates precisely the metaphysical determination of being as selfsame, noetic one. Referring to Heidegger's "uncircumventable meditation," Derrida identifies *différance*, in a certain way, with the epochal deployment of being, while also proposing that "in a certain and very strange way" it is older than being. Whether *différance* is thought in a way that exceeds even the beyond of Heideggerian thought is a question to which Derrida later returns again and again, and finally—though without any finality—in his book *Of Spirit: Heidegger and the Question*. He said it well in an interview with Richard Kearney in 1981: "Heidegger's texts are still before us; they harbor a future of meaning which will ensure that they are read and reread for centuries."[13]

But what, then—one will ask—is *différance*? In fact, this is precisely the question that was asked by one of the auditors, Brice Parain, in the discussion that followed Derrida's presentation of this text at the Sorbonne in 1968. Here is Parain's query: "Then, as you reached the main part of your lecture, I began to wonder what this *différance* might be, since, in short, it is the source of everything. It is the source of everything, and one cannot know it: it is the God of negative theology, and I understand very well. . . ." Here Derrida interrupted and said: "It is and it is not. . . . It is above all not. . . ." After some further questions by Parain, Derrida spoke directly to the question: "To ask about *différance* a question of origin or a question of essence, to ask oneself 'What is it?' is to return abruptly to the closure which I am attempting, with difficulty, laboriously and obliquely, to 'leave.'"[14] In other words, to ask about the

---

12. Ibid., 22.
13. Richard Kearney, *Dialogues with Contemporary Continental Thinkers* (Manchester: Manchester University Press, 1984), 110.
14. "The Original Discussion of '*Différance*' (1968)," trans. David Wood, Sarah Richmond, and Malcolm Bernard, in *Derrida and Différance*, ed. David Wood and Robert Bernasconi (Evanston, IL: Northwestern University Press, 1988), 84f.

"what," to pose the classical question τί ἐστι... ?, is to ask about the idea, about being in its metaphysical determination. The question would thus submit *différance* to precisely that which it is thought as exceeding.

It must be said, then, that *différance* is nothing present, that it is not a present being, neither in the sense of a sensible thing nor as the sense, the selfsame noetic one, that, shining through such things, renders them what they are, thus constituting (in the classical sense) their being. Derrida is explicit: "*Différance is not*, does not exist, is not a present being. ... It has neither existence nor essence"—nor (one may readily add) is it anything like an essence. He characterizes it, rather, as "opening the very space in which ... philosophy produces its system and its history," which it "exceeds without return." Thus, as he repeatedly insists, it is not a concept but rather "the possibility of conceptuality" as such.[15]

As the opening of the space of metaphysics, as the spacing that gives way to the founding distinction of metaphysics, *différance* displays an affinity to what Heidegger thinks as the clearing. What, on the other hand, most conspicuously distinguishes it is that it bundles or weaves together several senses of difference broached in earlier texts by Derrida, senses that, with the requisite precautions, could be called originary.

Among these ventures there is the deconstruction of the phenomenological theory of time-consciousness. Following Husserl's own descriptive analyses, Derrida shows that the present is not simply an absolute source-point of time. Rather, through retention and protention the present is linked to non-presence (past and future) *as* the very condition of its constitution. In other words, the present is produced through a compounding of presence and non-presence, through this distinctive operation of difference. Here is how Derrida describes it: "An interval must separate the present from what it is not in order for it to be itself; but this interval that constitutes it as present must, by the same token, divide the present in itself, thereby also dividing, along with the present, everything that is thought on the basis of the present, that is, in our metaphysical language, every being."[16] In other words, the production of the present occurs as a differencing of present from non-present that, at once, installs difference within the present, differencing it from itself. The operation of differencing is not something that supervenes upon an already constituted present but rather is the very production of the present, a differencing anterior to time itself—that is, *différance*.

15. Derrida, *Marges de la Philosophie*, 6, 11.
16. Ibid., 13.

Another earlier venture bundled in the sheaf of "La Différance" draws on Saussure's work, specifically on the role assigned to difference in the constitution of linguistic systems and the correlative thesis of the arbitrariness of the signifier. Derrida cites Saussure: "Everything up to this point comes down to saying that in language there are only differences. Even more important: a difference generally implies positive terms between which the difference is set up; but in language there are only differences *without positive terms*."[17] As in the constitution of time, linguistic signification is produced from an anterior operation of difference. Derrida puts it succinctly in *Of Grammatology*: "It is not a question here of a constituted difference, but rather, before all determination of the content, of the *pure* movement that produces difference. . . . Although it *does not exist*, although it is never a *being-present* outside of all plenitude, its possibility is by rights anterior to all that one calls sign."[18]

If *différance* is anterior to the operation of signification, then it likewise exceeds the νοητά of classical metaphysics to the extent that they are set out from—and thus inseparable from—λόγος. In any case, as the pure unifold determinacies that would shine forth in and determine the things of sense, they are disrupted by the submission of presence as such to the operation of *différance*. The things of nature as they are taken up in and through sense cannot, then, but be released, set free, set adrift, granted a plurality not again assimilable to being. In the wake of *différance*, nature is liberated.

As to difference itself—if there be an itself of difference—it will no longer—as *différance*—be either a form or a relation; it will no longer be subject to the categories of metaphysics. Even to call it the pure movement productive of categorial differences will remain inadequate, for movement denotes the movement of something, of some being, whereas with *différance* there is no being that moves. It retreats from the entire system of presence, precisely as it opens the space of this system. It cannot be integrated into the ontic-ontological circuit but withholds itself in what might well be called its disintegration. Its disintegration is the liberation of natural things to their unbounded plurality.

Thinking beyond being must let go of the beyond, must accede to its retreat from presence. Otherwise it will be drawn back into the ontic-ontological circuit; it will be misapprehended as being, and its advent will be mistaken for just another epoch—the latest—in the history

17. Ibid., 11.
18. Derrida, *De la Grammatologie* (Paris: Les Éditions de Minuit, 1967), 92.

of metaphysics. Its release will indeed serve for the releasement of the things of nature. In thinking beyond being there will also be carried out a return to the before of being, a return to natural things in their dispersion and unruliness. And yet, as it releases things, returning them to themselves, the beyond of being will itself prove elusive both to apprehension and to discourse. One will need to learn how to weave like Penelope.

Yet, among the ancients is it only this Homeric figure that displays an affinity with what is required of thinking beyond being? What if, on the contrary, in the ancient beginning of metaphysics the configuration of such thinking were already traced? What if, in this sense, the entire course of metaphysics were already enclosed within the beginning, or rather, were short-circuited in the beginning, and thus already, before having run its course, reached beyond its end? Would it not, then, be incumbent upon us to "think backwards," like the interlocutors in Heidegger's *Country Path Conversations*?[19] Would we not need to open ourselves to the possibility that the past might well come to meet us from out of the future, or that in returning to the beginning we might well find a way beyond the end?

It has not gone entirely unnoticed that thinking beyond being is enacted at certain junctures in the Platonic dialogues. In Heidegger's 1927 lecture course, *The Basic Problems of Phenomenology*, in which he sets out to develop the account of *Temporalität* that would have formed the third, missing division of *Being and Time*, he launches a discussion geared to Plato's *Republic*, in particular, to the discourse on the idea of the good. Observing that what illuminates knowledge both of beings and of being lies "beyond being," Heidegger says most pointedly: "The understanding of being is grounded in the projection of an ἐπέκεινα τῆς οὐσίας. Plato thus comes upon something that he describes as going beyond being."[20] In thinking *Temporalität* as the horizon from which being is understood, Heidegger would carry out a *Wiederholung* of this Platonic move.

The passage to which Heidegger alludes occurs in Book 6 of the *Republic*. At that point Socrates has just developed the analogy between the sun as it illuminates visible things and the good as it illuminates the

---

19. Heidegger, *Feldweg-Gespräche*, vol. 77 of *Gesamtausgabe* (Frankfurt a.M.: Vittorio Klostermann, 1995), 21.
20. Heidegger, *Die Grundprobleme der Phänomenologie*, vol. 24 of *Gesamtausgabe* (Frankfurt a.M.: Vittorio Klostermann, 1975), 402.

νοητά. Here is the pertinent passage: "Therefore, say that not only being known is present in the things known as a consequence of the good but also the 'to be' and being [τὸ εἶναί τε καὶ τὴν οὐσίαν] are in them besides as a result of it, although the good is not being but is still beyond being [ἐπέκεινα τῆς οὐσίας], exceeding it in dignity and power."[21] Thus, the very being of the νοητά, that they are as being, results from the good, as does also, consequently, the being of visible things, bestowed on them through the shining forth of the νοητά. But the good brings being about from beyond being, which it exceeds in dignity and power—that is, in πρεσβεία, which refers to the dignity or rank accorded to elders, which thus alludes to the anteriority of the good; also in δύναμις, in its capacity to affect, indeed to effect being as such. If one brings to bear on this passage the identification of being with δύναμις set forth in another Platonic text,[22] then it may be said that the good is the power of all powers, the very inception of power as such, of the power to set forth or to be set forth into presence.

In Book 7 there occurs, beginning with the image of the cave, a series of enactments, in various respects, of the move that, starting from visible images, ascends toward the good beyond being. Yet, when Glaucon entreats Socrates to lead him on to the τέλος of the ascent, Socrates replies that he would no longer be able to follow. He explains to Glaucon: "But you would no longer be seeing an image of what we are saying but rather the truth itself, at least as it appears to me. Whether it is really so or not can no longer be properly insisted on. But that there is some such thing to see must be insisted on."[23] In other words, even if they were to see beyond images to the beyond in its truth, they still would see it only *as it appears* to Socrates—that is, in still other images that would come to intervene. And so, Socrates insists only that there is such a beyond, even if it remains withdrawn behind its images. The passage is remarkable, especially in the way it unravels; it is as though Socrates were taking on the role of Penelope in order to image in this discursive enactment the elusiveness proper to the beyond of being.

There is another beyond of being that is thought in the Platonic dialogues, a kind that exceeds being, as it were, in the opposite direction. It is the beyond of being that is also the beginning before the beginning, that to which Timaeus is led when, making a new beginning, he unfolds

21. Plato, *Republic* 509b.
22. Plato, *Sophist* 247e.
23. Plato, *Republic* 533a.

his second discourse. Χώρα is what seems its most proper, or least improper, name among its many names. In his text so entitled, Derrida has called attention to the strangeness of the χώρα, to its being such that it cannot be assimilated to the ontic-ontological circuit. In another text he has also raised—and left unanswered, left as perhaps unanswerable—the question of why this beyond of being is never declared ἐπέκεινα τῆς οὐσίας and thus brought into its otherwise evident hyperontological affinity with the good. In Derrida's words: "And yet why does not Plato say that χώρα is ἐπέκεινα τῆς οὐσίας? Why is that so difficult to think?"[24]

In the *Timaeus* the χώρα is designated as a third kind (τρίτον γένος) in order to distinguish it from the first kind, which consists of the νοητά or εἴδη, and the second kind, which consists of visible things. And yet, even this designation unravels: since kinds are nothing other than εἴδη, any distinction between kinds occurs within the compass of the first kind, or, derivatively, of the second kind inasmuch as things image and are named after kinds of the first kind. The exteriority of the χώρα with respect to the ontic-ontological circuit—that is, its way of being beyond being—prohibits its being considered a kind, makes it a kind of kind beyond kind. This peculiar disconnection points to the enormous difficulty that will prove to be involved in thinking and saying the χώρα and that will prompt Timaeus to characterize the chorology as a bastard discourse. The elusiveness of the χώρα proves to render illegitimate whatever may nonetheless be said of it. Neither the χώρα nor the chorology can be *integrated* into the typology of kinds that structures the ontic-ontological sphere. Their abysmal difference sets them apart, *disintegrates* them.

Yet, the bearing of the χώρα on natural, visible things is utterly decisive. On the one hand, it is what allows things to possess a modicum of being. It is the nature before nature that gives place for nature. Timaeus explains: since any such thing "is always brought forth as the phantom of something other—because of this it is appropriate for it to be generated in something other, clinging to being at least in a certain way, on pain of being nothing at all."[25] By supplying an abode (ἕδρα) to all visible things, the χώρα lets them—in their limited, determined manner—be. Yet, on the other hand, their very dispersion in the χώρα—what

---

24. Derrida, "Tense," trans. D. F. Krell, in *The Path of Archaic Thinking: Unfolding the Work of John Sallis*, ed. Kenneth Maly (Albany: State University of New York Press, 1995), 73.

25. Plato, *Timaeus* 52c.

might be called the trace of the χώρα in them—is precisely what installs ἀνάγκη and discord in the domain of things. Yet this is to say, positively construed, that the χώρα is also what serves to withhold things from being, what detaches them from being utterly determined by the first kind and to this extent frees them. While this detachment is the source of much ill, most notably of illness and disease, it is also what makes plurality possible, both as multiplicity within each kind and as singularity unassimilable to the kind.

In the Platonic text there is to be found still another locus of thinking beyond being, a passage that in this regard has gone entirely unnoticed. A clue is provided by the chorological passage just cited, specifically by the double occurrence of the word ἕτερον (other or different): because things are phantoms of something *other*, they are to be generated in something *other*. What makes this double occurrence doubly intriguing is that one *other* is being itself, while the other *other* is most remote from being, most beyond being. Is there, then, within being somehow an other of being, a beyond of being within being?

This is the question that, in another, more general guise, is pursued in the *Sophist*, namely, as the question of how it is possible for non-being to be. As the Stranger formulates it: It is necessary to compel the λόγος "to say that non-being in some respects is and, in turn, that being in some way is not."[26]

The initial stage on this way involves patricide; it requires putting to the test the Parmenidean λόγος on the one being. In effect, what the Stranger demonstrates is that being cannot be constrained to being one, that, no matter how it is construed, the one being proves to be exceeded and thus proves not to be one. The demonstration is most direct as brought to bear on the very saying that being is one; for in this case there turn out to be two names for the same, and if there are two names, both being and one, then it is laughable to say that there is only one, that being is one. And so the demonstration proceeds until the thesis of one being must be withdrawn. What goes unmentioned is that this result pertains not only to Parmenides but also to the very account of being that, in the dramatic sequence, had been given on the previous day. For in the *Theaetetus* each being, each κοινόν or νοητόν, was determined as absolutely one with itself—that is, precisely as a one being. But now, with the result established by the Stranger, the beings can no longer be regarded simply and solely as ones, as countable. The stage is set for the

26. Plato, *Sophist* 241d.

discourse on the community (κοινωνία) of kinds, which displaces the previous day's discourse on the common (κοινόν). The discourse that proceeds on the community of five great kinds provides the context for the Stranger's discourse on the other (τὸ ἕτερον), that is, on difference as such.

The discussion of the five kinds traces the lines of the mixing and not mixing that form the configuration of the community. The Stranger points out, for instance, how motion is and is not the same. It is the same, as he says, "on account of its participation in the same in relation to itself."[27] In other words, by its participation in the same, it is the same as itself, is selfsame. This can indeed be said of all the kinds: that each is selfsame by participating in the same. Yet—decisively—this selfsameness does not exclude otherness or difference, for, as the Stranger says, "it is not the same on account of its sharing in the other."[28] In other words, by its participating in the other, motion is other than the same, hence is not the same. This, too, can be said of the other kinds: that each is other than the others by virtue of its participation in the other. In particular, each of the others is other than being itself by virtue of their participation in the other. Thus, it becomes evident that it is the other that has the effect of installing non-being in being. The Stranger is explicit: "So it is, after all, of necessity, in the case of motion and throughout all the kinds, that non-being be, for in each and every case the nature of the other, in producing each to be other than being, makes it non-being."[29] Thus, the Stranger effectively integrates non-being with being by doubling the sense of being. Yet, the question that goes unasked is whether within being there is not only non-being but also an exceeding of being, not an exceeding at the farthest extremes, as with the good and the χώρα, but an exceeding from within.

The integration of non-being with being is effected by means of the other. How is it, then, with the other itself, that is, with difference as such? Is there an itself of the other? Since it is a kind, it seems that, like the others, the other should be concentrated in a sameness with itself by participating in the same. And yet, the Stranger says, in fact twice, almost as if framing the heterology, that the other is *chopped into bits*. This is, in particular, the note on which the passage concludes: since each kind is other than every other kind by virtue of its participation in the

27. Ibid. 256b.
28. Ibid.
29. Ibid. 256d–e.

other, "the nature of the other both *is* and is chopped into bits and distributed through all beings in their relation to one another."³⁰

The Stranger does not elaborate but, instead, turns back to the general problem of non-being. But what he has said of the other implies contrast with the same. Each and every kind partakes of the same; yet the effect of this participation is to render each kind selfsame and hence also to set it apart from the same, leaving the same intact. If the same were said to partake of itself, such participation would only serve to reinforce its integrity: by participating in itself, the same would itself be selfsame.

But it is otherwise with the other. Each kind, while selfsame, is other than every other kind. Thus, each kind partakes multiply of the other. Each kind, of which there are many, participates in the other with respect to each and every other kind. It is to this proliferation of difference that the Stranger refers in saying that it is chopped into bits. It is as if it participated in itself so as to be other than itself, that is, dispersed, dismembered, disintegrated. But then, precisely in being the kind it is, it would be devoid of selfsameness and so would not be a kind. There would be a disintegration of difference at the very heart of being.

But how, finally, is the disintegration of difference—and, more broadly, the exceeding of being—carried over to the determination of the things of nature? Could it be that their differentiation, their spread, their spacing, exceeds—that is, escapes—ontological determination? Is there perhaps complicity between the disintegration of difference and the sense of spacing—the spacing of sense—that can be elaborated through a *Wiederholung* of the chorology? Could we, then, envision a spacing that would further the reimplacement of things amidst the elements? Could we, then, begin again, now at another beginning? Could we begin to think how, in their irreducible singularity and free plurality, the things of nature—and indeed we ourselves, too—occur amidst sunlight, wind, and rain, borne by the rhythm of the day and of the seasons, set within the broad enchorial space of earth and sky, and exposed to the boundless cosmos beyond?

---

30. Ibid. 258d–e.

ENGLISH INDEX

Abschattung, 79, 87. *See also* face/faces; profile
Alcibiades, 40
Anaximenes, 57
Andromeda, Nebula, 82, 84; Galaxy, 84, 87, 89
Aphrodite, 4
Apollo, 4, 102, 103; Apollinian, 70
appearance, 34, 55–56, 58, 61–63, 65, 67, 69–71, 82
Aristotle, 41, 56, 80, 100
Artemis, 4
Aufheben, 21, 22, 25
Augustine, 33

Beston, Henry, 8–9
beyng, 110
black hole, 57–58, 88–97
Brahe, Tycho, 82, 85, 91

Casey, Edward, 97
Cassiopeia, 82
causa sui, 36, 42
cepheid, 82–84
Christianity, 33, 65
Chrysippus, 45
clearing, 108–109, 112
community, 118
concealment, 4, 108
Copernicus, 83; Copernican Revolution, 49

deconstruction, 112
Derrida, Jacques, 92, 110, 112, 113, 116
Descartes, René, 31, 93
différance, 110–113
Diogenes: of Babylon, 45; of Sinope, 44

Emerson, Ralph Waldo, 11–18, 20, 49–50, 58
Empedocles, 30, 57, 75
Ereignis, 108
eros, 40

face/faces, 68
Feuerbach, Ludwig, 19
Fichte, J. G., 12, 20–21, 31, 34, 95, 100

Galilei, Galileo, 82–85, 87
German Idealism, 11–12, 18, 52, 99
God, 15–16, 18, 33–43, 65, 111; mind of, 14; nature of, 32

Harmony, 47–49
Hegel, G. W. F., 14, 19–24, 31, 35, 52, 75, 86; *Aesthetics*, 25–27
Heidegger, Martin, 92, 107–112; *The Basic Problems of Phenomenology*, 114; *Being and Time*, 55–56, 114; *Contributions to Philosophy*, 56; *Country Path Conversations*, 114
Heraclitus, 57
horizon, 59, 71–72, 78–79, 87, 90, 108, 114; event horizon, 57, 88–90 (*see also* black hole); horizonality, 71
Hotho, H. G., 25
Hubble, Edwin, 82–86
Husserl, Edmund, 85, 112

Imagination, 4, 34, 42–43; divine, 34; play of, 7; productive activity of, 26, 34; transcendental, 34; *true imagination*, 41
infinity, 34

122 ENGLISH INDEX

Jupiter, 82–83, 85, 87

Kant, Immanuel, 18, 20–21, 26, 93, 95, 100; *Critique of Judgment*, 13, 49; *Critique of Pure Reason*, 49, 56; and imagination, 34; transcendental idealism, 31
Klee, Paul, 99
Krell, David, 66

Leavitt, Henrietta, 83
l'état de nature, 45. See also state of nature
Lichtung, die, 108. See also clearing

Marx, Karl, 19, 107
Melody, 47–48
Merleau-Ponty, Maurice, 56
Metaphysics, 52, 56, 58, 93–94, 107–114; beginning of, 52, 105–106, 114; exhaustion of, 105, 107; history of, 55, 60, 92–97, 99–101, 105, 107; Nietzsche and, 58–72; overcoming of, 92
Michelangelo, 27
Mirandola, Pico della, 94

Nancy, Jean-Luc, 92
Neoplatonism, 100
Nietzsche, Friedrich, 54–55, 92–94, 107; *Beyond Good and Evil*, 68, 94; *The Birth of Tragedy*, 61, 70; *The Gay Science*, 68; inversion of Platonism, 58–72; *Thus Spoke Zarathustra*, 54, 65, 92. See also metaphysics: Nietzsche and

Parain, Brice, 111
Parmenides, 117
Pausanias, 75
Penelope, 4, 110, 114, 115
Pergolesi, 47
perspective, 68–72, 79, 87
Plato, 30–31, 40, 52–53, 68–69, 86, 92, 94, 109, 116; dialogues, 75, 95, 105, 114–115; and metaphysics, 58–72, 105; Platonism, 60–71; *Republic*, 95–96, 114; *Sophist*, 115n22, 117; *Symposium*, 40; *Theaetetus*, 105, 106, 117; *Timaeus*, 30,
31n2, 40n26, 53–57, 76, 81, 104, 115–116
Polemarchus, 96
polis, 81
Proclus, 96
profile, 71, 79

Rameau, Jean-Philippe, 47
Rousseau, Jean-Jacques, 18, 45–47; *Discourse on the Origin and Basis of Inequality among Men (Second Discourse)*, 45; *Essay on the Origin of Languages*, 47–48; *Letter on French Music*, 47; *The Wizard of the Village (Le Devin du Village)*, 48

Sartre, Jean-Paul, 97
Saussure, Ferdinand de, 113
Schein, 61, 69–70, 72. See also appearance
Schelling, Friedrich, 20–22, 29, 31–42, 52; idealism, 14, 99; *Ideas for a Philosophy of Nature*, 22; *On the Essence of Human Freedom*, 42, 52; *System of Transcendental Idealism*, 99
self-presence, 107
Shakespeare, William, 27
shining, 2, 69–72, 108–109, 112, 115, 112
space, 3, 11, 18, 22, 29, 76, 78, 88, 101, 108, 113; enchorial, 2, 58, 76, 78; free space, 110; for nature, 1; for the question, 94; of manifestation, 68; of metaphysics, 112; of a new beginning, 97; of a return, 50; of separation, 44
Spinoza, Baruch, 32
state of nature, 45–46, 48, 51, 81
Stobaeus, 45
Stoicism, 45

Thoreau, Henry David, 18, 51; *Walden*, 51
time, 6, 13, 37, 78–79, 112–113; horizon of, 108; time-consciousness, 112

unconcealment, 108

weaving/unweaving, 4, 110

Zeitlichkeit, 108

GREEK INDEX

ἀλήθεια, 108
ἀρχή, 30, 40, 43, 56, 105–107, 110

δημιουργός, 30, 53

εἶδος, 53, 76, 90–91, 109

ἰδέα, 106, 109

κοινωνία, 118

λόγος, 34, 91, 93, 105, 113, 117

ποίησις, 30, 39, 104

στοιχεῖα, 30, 76

τέχνη, 10

φύσις, 93

χώρα, 40, 53–54, 56, 76, 104, 116–118; sense of, 57

JOHN SALLIS is Frederick J. Adelmann Professor of Philosophy at Boston College. He is author of more than twenty books, including *Light Traces* (IUP, 2014) and *Logic of Imagination* (IUP, 2012).